What others a

Inves __ ..un
PURPOSE

Art, not only has the passion but the skill to present the Biblical Worldview of investing. He took me under his wing to learn about it and to execute Biblically Responsible Investing for my clients. This book captures those lessons and will answer the questions you may have not previously considered. I dare you to read this and not have a change of thinking about how you invest.

Barry R. James, CKA, CFA, CIC
President and CEO, James Investment Research Inc.

Invested with Purpose defines the "Timothy Family."

The Timothy Family has entered the "Promised Land Living and Thinking." They have witnessed the mighty hand of God parting the Jordan River to deliver them into the "Invested Purpose of the Kingdom of God." They are the body of Christ using their gifts, skills, and abilities to further the Kingdom of God. Art and Bonnie Ally have been the Joshua and Caleb leading God's people into the truth of God's invested purpose for all mankind and have been bold in their leadership for the righteousness and truth of the Gospel of Jesus Christ. *Invested with Purpose* is the testimony of God's redemptive plan of love and grace manifested in HIS FAMILY.

Glenn A. Repple, CLU, CFP®, EA
Founder & President, G.A. Repple & Company

While this book appears to be the story of a man, Art Ally, who is one of the finest, of highest-integrity people I know in the financial industry today, it is more about the movement that he began nearly a quarter of a century ago. It is about his faithfulness to God and his submission to the authority of Scripture and his Lord and Savior, Jesus Christ.

This is an amazing story of an amazing man, whose path was rocky and treacherous at times, but who never wavered. His love for his family, especially his dear wife and partner Bonnie, and his love for God, permeates this book which will become a catalyst for changing the way Christians invest. I cannot recommend it more highly.

Alan M. Ross
Founder and CEO, Kingdom Companies

Read this book!! Art Ally has literally laid it all (time, talent, and treasure) on the line as the main evangelist for what is now known as the Biblically Responsible Investment movement. When I first met Art at the second annual NACFC meeting, I wondered who is this guy who is judging me for where I am recommending clients to invest their money. I shortly found out!! He is a passionate follower of Jesus who believes, as I do, that you should put your money where your mouth is!!!

Art, congratulations on a great book (as if you had a choice once Patrice got hold of you). Art—write on...Public—read on.

Mick L. Owens, CFP®
Founder, The CFD Companies

No one has done more to illuminate the truth of Biblically Responsible Investing than Art Ally. This book, *Invested with Purpose*, is way overdue and a must-read for every Christian who desires to honor God in every aspect of their lives...including their investments.

Mark A. Minnella, CFS, CFCA
President, Integrity Investors, LLC

This book is an instruction manual for trusting the Lord with your finances. Art Ally shares his personal and professional stories that you can be faithful to the Lord and reap rewards on earth without compromise. I have chosen to be in alignment with his biblical investment strategies and now take confidence knowing my investments are sound before the Lord. The returns aren't bad either! I highly recommend you read this book and learn from his years of wisdom.

Dran Reese
President, The Salt and Light Council

Invested *with* PURPOSE

The Birth of the Biblically Responsible Investment Movement

ARTHUR D. ALLY

WITH ROBERT KNIGHT

Invested *with*
PURPOSE

Nehemiah Publishing
A Division of Nehemiah Project International Ministries, Inc.
5200 SW Meadows Rd, Suite 150,
Lake Oswego, OR 97035, U.S.A.
Phone: 877-916-1180
Fax: 503-726-5911
Printed in the U.S.A.
FIRST EDITION

Cover design and layout by Cheryl Mumbert.

Copy Editor: Charlie Nelson

ISBN: 978-1-940083-23-0

Library of Congress Control Number: 2019941909

DEDICATION

This book is dedicated to my wife Bonnie,
for putting up with me for nigh on 58 years,
and my children Doug, Steve, and Cheryl, who
have been integral parts of this project since
day one, as well as our entire staff of
outstanding team members supporting
Timothy Plan (i.e., Timothy Partners, Ltd.).

And in particular Stephen, our middle-born
son, who has valiantly battled cancer through
the entire time of writing this book. You're an
inspiration to all of us.

ACKNOWLEDGEMENTS

I want to thank all our financial partners of Timothy Partners, Ltd. who put up the money for this project; our Timothy Plan Trustees, who faithfully meet quarterly to exercise oversight, and all our Money Management Sub-Advisors as well as all the other moving parts and pieces that make what we do possible: Ultimus Fund Solutions, which provides back-office support; Investment Industry Services Division of Cohen & Company, who have been our auditors for years; our Fund Counsel, David Jones, our Custodian Bank, U.S. Bank, and especially our Institutional Consultants: Allen, Kevin and Kristi. Also, my favorite nationally renowned financial radio host, Dan Celia, who is more like a twin brother than a friend due to his commitment to Biblical Principles as well as Biblically Responsible Investing. Finally, I want to thank Patrice Tsague for steering this project into life, my daughter Cheryl for the cover, graphic design and layout, and Robert Knight for helping me to communicate what Biblically Responsible Investing is all about.

Contents

Preface

Patrice Tsague

I came to know Art Ally at a Christian business conference in 2007. We both had one thing in common: a commitment to see Biblical values lived out in the marketplace—for him in the investment world, for me in managing a business. Since then, he's become like a father to me—an advisor, an inspiration, a benefactor, and when necessary, someone who challenges me.

"Invested with Purpose" is not just another business or investment book. It's the account of the miraculous journey of one man who led by conviction and a determination to obey God. Art sparked a movement that has created a multi-billion-dollar sub-industry in financial services. The book takes you from a near shutdown of Timothy Plan's advisor on a New Year's Eve Day to the development of the growing movement called Biblically Responsible Investing.

It's our hope that you will be inspired by Art's journey in building Timothy Plan, the pioneer in Biblically Responsible Investing. We also hope you will be challenged to be Invested with Purpose while making a difference not just with your finances but in your own industry and community.

Truth be told, Art didn't really want to write this book and agreed only after he was convinced of its potential impact to our nation, the Kingdom and future generations. We worked very hard to make sure the book reflects Art's passion, vision, intensity and bluntness. You will be inspired, encouraged, empowered, perhaps even offended. But, in the end, we hope you will be moved to action to be Invested with Purpose toward realizing God's plan for your life.

Art Ally has modeled for us how to live a purposeful life with conviction, determination, faithfulness and generosity. Special thanks to Robert Knight for partnering with us as the wise scribe to bring this life-transforming story to life.

May you be inspired by it to live a purposeful life for God's glory.

Patrice Tsague
Founder and Chief Servant Officer
Nehemiah Project International Ministries
Publisher

Foreword
Belief and Real Hope

Often, our modern cultural gurus tell us that it doesn't matter what you believe as long as you believe in something.

But that's a misconception. It replaces truth with relativism, the idea that we can make up our own "truth" to suit our needs and desires. This is the fundamental philosophy taught at nearly all colleges and universities, and which trickles down to the K-12 schools. Popular culture plays this tune constantly.

Christians are not immune to this siren song. If not fortified and educated by biblically sound pastors, we're apt to absorb the many relativistic and hedonistic messages around us. As such, we're tempted to act and think not very differently from people with a pagan worldview, especially when it comes to spending and investing money. As Art Ally would say, our first mistake is thinking the money we have is ours—not God's.

Jesus predicted an era like the one we are in—

For the time will come when they will not endure sound doctrine, but according to their own desires, because they have itching ears, they will heap up for themselves teachers; and they will turn their ears away from the truth, and be turned aside to fables.—2 Timothy 4, 3-4

Modern paganism teaches that humans were not created by God but merely evolved by chance; that morality is a vestige of an oppressive, obsolete belief system and that therefore right and wrong are in the mind of the beholder. Ironically, many modern pagans who promote relativism believe religiously in non-negotiable items like sexual anarchy, manmade climate change, and forced economic redistribution, all with a need for heavy government enforcement.

So where does this leave believing Christians?

According to pollster George Barna, only nine percent of American adults have a biblical worldview,[i] and only 17 percent of regular churchgoers have a biblical worldview.[ii]

Here is a summary of basic Christian doctrine:

1) God is timeless and created the universe and everything in it;
2) He created the Earth as a place for his crowning creation—man—to flourish;
3) He created male and female in His own image and joined them in marriage;
4) Adam and Eve were tempted by Satan, a fallen angel, into sin. This brought death into the world, a circumstance still afflicting us;
5) Jesus was born into the world as fully God and fully man 2,000 years ago as not only the prophesied Messiah in Scripture to the Jewish people but as the Lamb of God Who was

to be sacrificed for the sins of the whole world.

6) Jesus was crucified, was buried and rose on the third day.

7) Before departing for Heaven, He appeared before hundreds of people, including His disciples and several devoted women followers, and promised eternal life to all who believe in Him.

8) At His appointed time, Jesus will return amid a new Heaven and a new Earth. He will destroy all evil and gather all of his spiritual children who will live forever with Him in Heaven.

There is much more, of course. The Bible's 1,700-plus pages contain an unparalleled collection of wisdom, teaching, history, and theology. But the above is the bare minimum for a biblical worldview.

Who Calls the Shots?

America is in trouble today because we have left these beliefs—and the Bible—behind and have pursued our own interests as we see them, meaning we call the shots, not God. For many people, God has become, at best, a sort of consultant—until He gets in the way of our plans. Then we seek out other sources of enlightened excuses for our behavior.

The Scriptures are replete with warnings about pride being our downfall, beginning with Adam and Eve's rebellion at the dawn of humanity—

There is a way that seems right to a man, but its end is the way of death.—Proverbs 14:12

The more that our culture drifts from a biblically-grounded worldview, the worse our consequences. Perhaps drift is the wrong word. We have been running pell-mell from our Christian heritage at breakneck speed over the last few decades.

In Matthew 28: 19-20, Jesus gave the Great Commission:

"Go therefore and make disciples of all nations, baptizing them in the name of the Father and of the Son and of the Holy Spirit, teaching them to observe all that I have commanded you. And behold, I am with you always, to the end of the age."

Revealing how lukewarm the church has become, Barna Group found that nearly half of Christian Millennials directly reject the Great Commission, agreeing that: "It is wrong to share one's personal beliefs with someone of a different faith in hopes that they will one day share the same faith."[iii]

Christians of all people should boldly shine with the hope within us due to the presence of the Holy Spirit and the knowledge that God loves us. To borrow a well-worn phrase, it is better to light a candle than to curse the darkness. The Spirit should permeate everything we do, including how we handle our money—a topic the Bible addresses in more than 2,300 verses.

A Clear Vision

In 1994, Art Ally lit a candle in the darkness: Timothy Plan.

This book is an attempt to encapsulate what that's meant to so many and continues to mean. As the pioneer of Biblically Responsible Investing (BRI), Art has been used by God to give Christians a way to invest our money without unwittingly aiding immoral causes.

Timothy Plan's mission is strikingly simple—

Being "committed to maintaining portfolios that do not contain the securities of any company that is promoting an agenda contrary to the teachings of scripture, or is actively participating in activities that may prove destructive to our communities at large."

Art has inspired many to embrace BRI, which not only deprives evil doers of support but allows us to better provide for our families and to give to ministries and other good causes, just as Timothy Partners does (see the chapter on Giving Back).

Whatever else we get out of this account of the birth and growth of Timothy Plan, Art is adamant for us to understand this:

Timothy Plan was never his plan...
it was God's.

Robert Knight

---

[i] Barna Group, "Changes in Worldview Among Christians over the Past 13 Years," March 9, 2009, at barna.com/research/barna-survey-examines-changes-in-worldview-among-christians-over-the-past-13-years.

[ii] Barna Group, "Competing Worldviews Influence Today's Christians," May 9, 2017, at barna.com/research/competing-worldviews-influence-todays-christians

[iii] "Almost Half of Practicing Christian Millennials Say Evangelism Is Wrong," Faith and Christianity articles, Barna Group, Feb. 5, 2019, at barna.com/research/millennials-oppose-evangelism

IMPORTANT INFORMATION

①

A New Year's Eve
to Remember

Not only so, but we also glory in our sufferings, because
we know that suffering produces perseverance;
—Romans 5:3

> We're excited you are on this journey with us to learn
> how to be Invested with Purpose. This is the story of
> a fledgling mutual fund that gave birth to a movement
> which revolutionized the financial services industry.

Biblically Responsible Investing is not only a financial strategy but also a way of life based on the teachings of the Bible. This book chronicles how one man's obedience has resulted in Timothy Plan shifting more than $1 Billion of assets away from companies engaged in activities not consistent with biblical values. This story almost did not end well and could have ended quickly if not for God's intervention and guidance. This first chapter relates one such incident.

On New Year's Eve, 2002, Art Ally came into the office in the early afternoon. It was a Friday, and a few people were at their desks, nervously going about their business and trying to ignore the ticking clock on the wall.

Timothy Plan's distributor had been operating for eight years and had narrowly escaped bankruptcy three times.

"We were on a skeleton crew," remembered Dave Hart, the newly hired advisor relations director. "I asked Art, 'What are you doing here?'

"He said, 'If we don't make net capital by 4 o'clock today, I guess we're going to have to shut her down.'

"I asked, 'What are you going to do?' He responded, 'Nothing, I've already done my job.' Then he walked into his office, sat down, and I heard him playing Bridge Baron on his computer."

The staff wasn't sure what to make of this. How could Art be so calm with doom quickly approaching?

"I did not venture into his office because I was dialing as many brokers as possible," Steve Ally, Art's son, recalled.

"Some folks were anxious. Dave Hart was anxious. However, Art—he was cool as a cucumber; there was no stress. Art had no worries at all. He had full faith something was going to happen. Whatever it was, it was the Lord's will."

Amidst the worry, everyone was quietly praying.

"We were upstairs in the old building, and we were having a discussion

in Art's office," relates Terry Covert, who served as representative to pastors. "I can remember when I said, 'You know, Art, this may come down to where the only employees are you and Bonnie. You may have to close the office and run it out of your bedroom. It is going to be successful, just not as fast as we thought it would be.'"

Indeed, right before 4, the phone rang in Art's office. "I was standing in his office when he received the call," Terry said. "He hung up the phone and said something to the effect that God had done it."

"I heard him slap his hands together," Dave reports. "Whenever anything good happened, I'd always hear him slap his hands and rub them together."

Minutes later, Art walked out smiling. "Well, God did His job. It's at the 11th hour, but He did it."

A partner had called and pledged another $400,000 in capital to keep Timothy Plan's distributor going.

Bonnie and daughter Cheryl were in an office downstairs. "It was so quiet in the office," Cheryl recalled. "There was a big sigh of relief."

Terry recollects, like Art, he wasn't particularly anxious that day. "You figured God's will was going to be done one way or the other. It was a big deal when the money came in because it reaffirmed what we were doing."

For Art, it was a turning point. "I knew then I could be comfortable trusting God since He could have shut us down anytime in the preceding eight years. Instead, He forced us through a keyhole four times. The lesson is, we can trust God—and He has to know, He can trust us."

Do you have your own New Year's Eve story? Do you remember that moment in your life when the purpose you felt called to accomplish almost came to an end? May Timothy Plan's story inspire and encourage you to continue for the glory of God.

Money as a Soul Concern

*What good will it be for someone to gain the whole
world, yet forfeit their soul? Or what can anyone give in
exchange for their soul?—Matthew 16:26*

In our journey to be Invested with Purpose, we must
make sure we have the right priorities. Many begin
with proper motives but eventually compromise over
financial gain or lack thereof. The Bible states money
(or mammon) has the potential to compete directly
with Almighty God for our loyalty. We must choose now
which master we will serve before we get too far into our
journey. If not, we'll find ourselves turning money into
our master. Whether we're in business, a professional
career, or nonprofit service, we can all become victims
of mammon's temptations—especially those of us in
financial services. We must make sure we pursue our

purpose with the right motives and that we have the right attitude about money. The Bible warns us about those whose sole purpose is acquiring riches instead of service to others and honoring God.

Those who want to get rich fall into temptation and a trap and into many foolish and harmful desires that plunge people into ruin and destruction.—I Timothy 6:9

One of the most revealing areas of life is how we handle money. If we think it's all ours, we approach it differently than if we realize God owns everything and we're merely stewards of the riches He has allowed us to earn.

The Scriptures contain more than 2,300 verses referencing money, far more even than the topic of faith (600 verses). Jesus devoted more than 15 percent of his recorded words to this subject. How we handle money reflects what we really believe.

As Jesus said—

But store up for yourselves treasures in heaven, where neither moth nor rust destroys, and where thieves do not break in or steal; for where your treasure is, there your heart will be also.—Matthew 6:20-21

A fair reading of Jesus' comments shows He neither recommended asceticism (complete rejection of the material world) nor the opposite error, materialism (a preoccupation with wealth, sensations, and material things).

The Apostle Paul criticized asceticism this way—

For everything created by God is good, and nothing is to be rejected if it is received with thanksgiving, for it is made holy by the word of God and prayer.—1 Timothy 4:4,5

Honest work is not only honorable, but as we are told in the Book of Proverbs, integral to one's wellbeing—

Go to the ant, you sluggard! Consider her ways and be wise, which, having no captain, overseer or ruler, provides her supplies in the summer, and gathers her food in the harvest.—Proverbs 6:6-8

Prepare your outside work, make it fit for yourself in the field; and afterward build your house.—Proverbs 24:27

On the other side of the coin, Jesus warned against materialism in any form and in any era—

Beware, and be on your guard against every form of greed; for not even when one has an abundance does his life consist of his possessions.—Luke 12:15

Jesus also made it clear material wealth can become an idol in itself and prevent people from seeking the most considerable wealth of all—a deep relationship with a loving God—

It is easier for a camel to go through the eye of a needle than for a rich person to enter the kingdom of God.—Mark 10:25

The problem is not money, but the love of money, as the apostle Paul noted famously in 1 Timothy—

For the love of money is a root of all kinds of evils.
It is through this craving that some have wandered
away from the faith and pierced themselves with many
pangs.— 1 Timothy 6:10

A Barna Group study found, the richer people get, the less likely they are to commit to following Jesus: "Those making more than $100K per year are significantly less likely (53%) to have made such a commitment than those making between $50K and $100K (63%) or those making less than $50K (65%)."[1]

It's not better to be materially poor or wrong to be rich. Many Bible verses instruct about diligently earning a living and investing to increase one's wealth. Without at least some wealth, we could not care for our families and give to the church and to those in need. Properly understood, the more we make, the more we can bless others.

What we should not do is fall into debt. It makes it more difficult for us to be a blessing to others.

> What is your attitude toward money? Are you its master, or does it master you? Remember, money cannot be our sole concern and must be a soul concern. Our primary goal is to be good stewards for the Kingdom of God. If not, it can wreck our purpose.

[1] Barna Group, "What Do People Believe about Jesus? 5 Popular Beliefs," April 1, 2015, at barna. com/research/what-do-americans-believe-about-jesus-5-popular-beliefs

3

The Wages of Debt

The rich rule over the poor, and the borrower is slave to the lender.—Proverbs 22:7

> Debt is an enemy of a purposeful life. It robs us of our margin, holds us back from our passion, and threatens our loyalty to God. In fact, debt may well pose the greatest threat to our being Invested with Purpose. Even the United States of America, a great superpower, risks its national security due to uncontrolled debt.

The Bible is full of warnings about spending too much. Proverbs informs us—

The borrower is slave to the lender.—Proverbs 22:7b

In Romans, Paul admonishes—

*Let no debt remain outstanding, except for the continu-
ing debt to love one another, for he who loves his fellow-
man has fulfilled the law.—Romans 13:8*

Living Beyond Our Means

If we find we need to borrow, we should have a plan to pay it back
sooner than the period of the loan. Otherwise, we wind up paying
far more than the original cost. The most striking example is the
National Debt of the United States.

The USDebtClock.org, which tracks America's rising debt at diz-
zying speed, was introduced on February 20, 1989, by New York
real estate mogul Seymour Durst. The clock began by reporting a
national debt of "only" $2.7 trillion.[1]

By 1991, it was increasing at $13,000 per second. In fact, it "began
accumulating so fast that the last seven digits became totally illegi-
ble," Time magazine reported.[2]

The clock actually broke in 1998 because it couldn't handle the
total of $5.5 trillion. In 2008, a digit was added because the debt
had grown to $10 trillion.[3] Over the next eight years, the nation's
debt rose to more than $20 trillion, and today it is past $22 trillion.

Trillion has become a meaningless word to most people. It's an
astronomically high figure, with 12 zeros. Bear in mind, a billion
is one thousand million. If you had a machine printing dollar bills,
and it printed a dollar every second, 60 seconds a minute, 60 minutes an hour, 24 hours a day, and 365 days a year, do you know how
long it would take that machine to print $1 trillion? Cranking non-
stop, it would take more than 31,709 years.

Why is this important? Because the government is living beyond its means, and we're all paying interest on the debt, which compounds, creating more debt. The obligation for each individual taxpayer, as of March 2019, now exceeds $223,000, and the total debt per family is upwards of $868,000.[4]

Who will pay for all of this? Our children and grandchildren.

The Bible is specific, piling up debt is a dereliction of duty—

> For the children ought not to lay up for the parents, but the parents for the children.—2 Corinthians 12:14

Paul says parents should provide for their children and not weigh them down with debt.

The Lure of Credit Cards

Personal credit card debt is out of control for millions of people.

The average American had a credit card balance of $5,331 in March 2019, according to TheStreet.com.[5] Total average household debt neared $50,000 in 2018, according to the Federal Reserve, not including a home mortgage.[6]

Americans with education debt "owe between $20,000 and $25,000 on average." CNBC reports.[7]

God's Economy vs. the World's

Problems with debt begin in the human heart, Scripture informs us—

> Watch out! Be on your guard against all kinds of greed," Jesus told a crowd. "Life does not consist in an abundance of possessions.—Luke 12:15

Author Randy Alcorn notes that wanting ever more material goods contrasts with a forward-looking, eternal outlook in which trusting God and giving back to Him is more important. In God's economy, giving is the coin of the realm—not getting.

Debt keeps us from giving our best to our Creator, Who, after all, owns everything.

Many Bad Outcomes

There are many consequences of a debt-laden lifestyle.

DEBT:

- lingers
- causes worry and stress
- causes denial of reality
- leads to dishonesty
- is addictive
- is presumptuous
- deprives God of the chance to say no or to provide through a better means
- is a significant loss of opportunity
- ties up resources, making them unavailable for the Kingdom of God[8]

Instead of striving for more worldly acquisitions, we should follow the advice of Jesus, who said—

> But seek first His kingdom, and His righteousness, and all these things will be given to you as well.—Matthew 6:33

It comes down to trusting God's provision rather than the empty material promises of the world.

When we are able, we need to save money and invest wisely—but not in ventures promoting immorality. Everything we do should advance God's Kingdom.

Speaking of investing, let's look next at what the Bible has to say.

> How well do you have your finances under control? Are you free from debt? Remember, we will never experience real freedom if we are bound by debt. Our purpose will be compromised if our obligations are out of control. Being Invested with Purpose is a path to freedom. To the contrary, indebtedness can rob us of freedom.

[1] M.J. Stephey, "The Times Square Debt Clock," *Time* magazine, Oct. 14, 2008, at content.time.com/time/business/article/0,8599,1850269,00.html.
[2] Ibid.
[3] Ibid.
[4] USdebtclock.org.
[5] Brian O'Connell, "What's the Average U.S. Credit Card Debt by Income and Age in 2019?" TheStreet.com, Feb. 16, 2019, at thestreet.com/personal-finance/credit-cards/average-credit-card-debt-14863601.
[6] Alan Kline, "Household debt hit another all-time high. Is it poised to level off?" AmericanBanker.com, Feb. 19, 2019, at americanbanker.com/list/household-debt-hit-another-all-time-high-is-it-poised-to-level-off.
[7] Abigail Hess, "US student debt levels set a new record in 2018—here's how much the typical borrower owes," CNBC, Dec. 28, 2018, at cnbc.com/2018/12/27/student-debt-levels-set-a-new-record-in-2018-heres-how-much-the-typical-borrower-owes.html.
[8] Listed under Consequences in the Debt chapter, "Stewardship: God's Plan for Financial Success, Family Edition," (Orlando: Timothy Plan, 2004, updated most recently in 2017), p. 34.

What Is Biblically Responsible Investing?

"Come out from among them and be separate," says the LORD. "Do not touch what is unclean, and I will receive you."—2 Corinthians 6:17

Knowing the value of being debt-free, let's talk about the proper view of investing the margins (e.g., disposable income). Freedom from debt combined with purposeful work produces margins. What do we do with those margins? We ought to be saving and investing. To be Invested with Purpose, we must approach investing differently; we cannot benefit from the very things that destroy our values and convictions. Who we are as Christians must be reflected not only in how we worship in community, live our lives, and work, but also in how we invest our money. Let's look at the history of what shaped the idea of investing biblically.

You don't have to be a Christian to want to invest your money in companies that make the world a better—not worse—place. Christians and Jews have additional insight through the Scriptures that all of our money—and our time—belongs to God, not just the amount we tithe, or the time we spend in worship.

The Origins of BRI

The field of Biblically Responsible Investing is not new; God gave us the blueprint from the very beginning. The current application happens to revolve around modern investment opportunities.

Genesis 1 through 3 tells us God created all things, including men and women, for His own glory, and human beings are at the very top of His creative order. This means human beings, while inherently sinful, are beloved by God and should be treated with dignity, respect, and compassion. Everything we do needs to take that into account, including our investments. We should vigorously avoid ventures that traffic in sin and thus are destructive to people.

Good stewardship begins with an acknowledgment of Who is the real Chairman of the Board:

"I believe the most dangerous misconception is the idea our money and possessions belong to us, not God," says Randy Alcorn, author, and founder of Eternal Perspective Ministries. "Many of our problems begin when we forget that God is the Boss of the universe. In fact, He is more than the boss; He is the owner."[1]

From beginning to end, Scripture repeatedly emphasizes God's ownership of everything—

To the Lord your God belong the heavens, even the highest heavens, the earth and everything in it—Deuteronomy 10:14.[2]

"When I grasp that I'm a steward, not an owner, it totally changes my perspective. Suddenly, I'm not asking, 'How much of my money shall I, out of the goodness of my heart, give to God?' Rather, I'm asking, 'Since all of 'my' money is really yours, Lord, how would you like me to invest your money today?'"[3]

Real Security

Scripture often reminds us that while money is essential, our security, both earthly and eternal, lies in our relationship with God—

And you shall remember the Lord your God, for it is He who gives you power to get wealth, that He may establish His covenant which He swore to your fathers, as it is this day.—Deuteronomy 8:18

And my God shall supply all your need according to His riches in glory by Christ Jesus.—Philippians 4:19

The Bible places much importance on how wealth is accumulated—

Better is a little with righteousness, than vast revenues without justice.—Proverbs 16:8

Jesus Himself put it more starkly—

For what profit is it to a man if he gains the whole world, and loses his own soul?—Matthew 16:26

Christians and
Biblically Responsible Investing

Throughout history, Christians have promoted one form or another of biblically responsible economic activity.

In 1524, Christian reformer Martin Luther excoriated businessmen who left out ethics: "The merchants have a common rule... I shall sell my wares as dear as I can... But it means making room for greed and opening the door and window of hell... so long as I have my profit and satisfy my greed, of what concern is it to me if it injures my neighbor in ten ways at once? So you see how this motto goes so straight and shamelessly against not only Christian love but also natural law as well."[4]

John Wesley (1703-1791), the founder of the Methodist movement, "urged his followers to shun profiting at the expense of their neighbors. Consequently, they avoided partnering or investing with those who earned their money through alcohol, tobacco, weapons, or gambling—essentially establishing social investment screens."[5]

Before the United States became an independent nation, English-born New Jersey tailor John Woolman (1720-1772) refused to buy any cotton or dye handled by slaves.

"What pious man could be a witness to these things, and see a trade carried on in this manner, without being deeply affected with sorrow?" he wrote.[6] "Through abiding in the love of Christ, we feel a tenderness in our hearts toward our fellow creatures entangled in oppressive customs; and a concern so to walk that our conduct may not be a means of strength'ning them in error. It was the command of the Lord through Moses, thou shalt not suffer sin upon thy brother."[7]

In 1759, Woolman persuaded the Quakers in Philadelphia to pass the first resolution in the colonies prohibiting participation in any aspect of the slave trade,[8] presaging the Abolitionist Movement that led to the Civil War (1861-1865).

The 20th Century and Beyond

In 1928, Philip Carret launched the Fidelity Mutual Trust, which became the Pioneer Fund, one of the first-ever mutual funds. Designed initially to serve church investors, the fund had a policy of "screening investments on ethical grounds," rejecting companies which traded in alcohol or tobacco. The fund survived the Great Depression and went on to become one of the largest mutual funds. [9] Recalling Carret, who died at age 101 in 1998, Warren Buffet said, "Phil was a hero of mine. He had the best long-term investment record of anyone I know."[10]

In 1976, Larry Burkett founded Christian Financial Concepts (CFC), teaching people biblical financial management as part of an overarching life plan. In 2000, CFC merged with Crown Ministries, founded by Howard Dayton in 1985. This ministry is similar to that of the Christian radio talk show host Dave Ramsey, encouraging people to get out of debt and live within defined budgets.

In 1989, Tom Strobhar, a pro-life investment advisor in Dayton, Ohio, began buying a few shares in 25 corporations so he could attend stockholder meetings and lobby management against donating to Planned Parenthood, investing in pornography or promoting immoral lifestyles. "Folks like Timothy Plan have made [abortion] an issue, so it has worked," Mr. Strobhar explained in an interview. He mentioned that at least 340 companies which formerly gave to Planned Parenthood have ceased doing so.[11] Mr. Strobhar authored the first shareholder resolutions against child pornography, religious bigotry, fetal tissue research, and abortifacients.[12]

Don't Confuse BRI with SRI

A lot of people tuck Biblically Responsible Investing (BRI) under the umbrella of Socially Responsible Investing (SRI), or Sustainable, Responsible, and Impact Investing, but that's misleading.

Both SRI and BRI employ screening criteria; however, each screen for different things and in different ways, as they have differing agendas. In general, SRI encourages corporate practices to promote environmental stewardship, consumer protection, human rights, and diversity. Some avoid businesses involved in alcohol, tobacco, weapons, fossil fuel production, or the military.[13] The areas of concern recognized by the SRI practitioners are sometimes summarized under the heading of ESG issues: environment, social justice, and corporate governance.

A BRI fund is a place for Christian investors to invest their money, knowing their investments are not supporting companies that contradict a traditional biblical ethic. Timothy Plan's BRI portfolio screens out "sin stocks," which violate God's rules for living. This means excluding companies trading in or supporting abortion, pornography, gambling, anti-family entertainment, tobacco and alcohol, unbiblical lifestyles, human oppression, human trafficking, slave labor, terrorism, and Christian persecution.

> How are you currently managing your investments? Did you know some investments support the very things that contradict your values?

[1] Christ-Centered Stewardship in a Consumer-Driven Culture: An Interview about Money and Giving," Eternal Perspective Ministries, July 5, 2017, at epm.org/blog/2017/Jul/5/christ-centered-stewardship.

[2] Ibid.

[3] Ibid.

[4] Martin Luther, "Price Fixing by Commission," in Walton Hale Hamilton, editor, Current Economic Problems: A Series of Readings in the Control of Industrial Development (Chicago: The University of Chicago Press, 1915), p. 158.

[5] William Donovan, "A Short History of Socially Responsible Investing," The Balance, February 7, 2018, at thebalance.com/a-short-history-of-socially-responsible-investing-3025578.

[6] John Woolman, "On the Slave Trade," in Amelia Mott Gummere, editor, The Journal and Essays of John Woolman, (Philadelphia: Friends' Bookstore, 1922) pp. 496-503, at qhpress.org/texts/oldqwhp/wool-496.

[7] Ibid.

[8] Ibid.

[9] Mary Naber, "Christ's Returns: Building an Investment Plan Beyond Profit," Christianity Today, September 3, 2001, p. 79.

[10] Quoted in Bud Labitan, The Four Filters Invention of Warren Buffett and Charlie Munger, copyright 2014 by Bud Labitan, p. 178.

[11] Tom Strobhar, telephone interview with Robert Knight on March 13, 2018.

[12] Strobhar Financial website at strobharfinancial.org/about.htm.

[13] C. Logue, Ann. Socially Responsible Investing For Dummies. Wiley.com. p. 196.

Mutual Funds: Investments for the People

Again, it will be like a man going on a journey, who called his servants and entrusted his wealth to them.
—Matthew 25:14

> No matter our situation, most of us who live in America have been entrusted with much. The question is, are we stewarding it faithfully? One way to faithfully steward the finances with which the Lord has entrusted us is through mutual funds. Since we're committed to being Invested with Purpose, we must make sure that the mutual funds we use are biblically responsible.

Truett Cathy, the late, great founder of Chick-fil-A, liked to say, "We didn't invent the chicken, just the chicken sandwich."

He would then give credit to the Lord for his company's success.

In a similar way, we can say Timothy Plan didn't invent mutual funds, but it did pioneer the concept of Biblically Responsible Investing. Biblically Responsible Investing is executed through a mutual fund strategy accessible to a majority of people.

Mutual funds, or something like them, go way back to the 18th Century.

We owe the Dutch for coming up with the concept of pooled capital to acquire assets for investing: *negotiaties*—the essence of today's mutual funds.

A merchant, Abraham van Ketwich, is generally credited with creating the first such instrument in 1774. Just as mutual funds aid millions of people today who are not wealthy to access investment markets, Mr. van Ketwich designed his new vehicle for people of modest means.

The name of the first fund, Eendragt Maakt Magt, translates to "unity creates strength." It was assembled from foreign government bonds and plantation loans in the New World—specifically, in the West Indies.[1]

The success of what was called a *negotiatie* encouraged Mr. van Ketwich to form other such funds, with one of them lasting more than 114 years before being dissolved.[2] Other merchants and traders created their own *negotiaties*, and the concept spread all over Europe and even into North America. During the 1780s, more than 30 *negotiaties* owned United States credit issues alone.

In Switzerland, an investment trust was launched in 1849, with more created in Scotland during the 1880s.[3] In 1893, The Boston Personal Property Trust was America's first closed-end fund, followed by others. The Alexander Fund was the first to allow investors to make withdrawals on demand.[4]

Fast forward to the Roaring Twenties, and two more important developments occurred. Scudder, Stevens, and Clark launched the first no-load fund in America in 1928, while the Wellington Fund was the first mutual fund to include stocks and bonds. According to Investopedia, "By 1929, there were 19 open-ended mutual funds competing with nearly 700 closed-end funds" before the stock market crashed in 1929 and ushered in the Great Depression.[5]

The federal Securities and Exchange Commission was created in 1934 to protect investors, followed by the Securities and Exchange Act of 1940, which introduced regulatory oversight of mutual funds and registered investment advisors.

Over the years, the mutual fund industry fluctuated with the markets but rose steadily toward today's financial scene, in which some 14,000 funds operate.

Wells Fargo created the first index fund in 1971, the same year the first money market fund—The Reserve Fund—was established. Vanguard's John Bogle opened the 500 Portfolio of Vanguard Index Trust (initially operating under the name First Index Investment Trust) in 1974, allowing small investors to participate.

Meanwhile, the creation of IRA and 401(k) retirement accounts began replacing traditional pension plans, mainly through mutual funds. This "democratized" investments, as people from every economic segment, not just the wealthy, began acquiring a stake in the markets—a modern-day application of Mr. van Ketwich's vision.

What is a Mutual Fund

A mutual fund is a type of investment vehicle (a registered investment company) that sells shares, and by doing so, accumulates a pool of money collected from many investors. The pool is invested in securities such as stocks, bonds, money market instruments, other assets, and sometimes a combination of the various investments. Mutual fund daily activities are conducted by professional money managers, who allocate the fund's assets and attempt to produce capital gains, income, or a combination of the two for the fund's investors.

Mutual funds are sold by prospectus; the prospectus provides extensive information about the fund's management, goals, risks, structure, history, and other information that provides investors with extensive knowledge about the fund. Each fund's portfolio is structured, selected, and maintained to match investment objectives published in its prospectus.

By investing in mutual funds, small or individual investors can be diversified while gaining access to professionally managed portfolios of stocks, bonds, and other securities. Performance is usually tracked as the change in the total value (up or down) of the underlying assets being held in the fund, plus dividends and capital gains earned by the fund. Each shareholder participates in the gains or losses of the fund.

Exchange-Traded Funds

While the majority of mutual funds are actively managed by professional money management firms, most Exchange-Traded Funds (ETFs) are passive investments that typically track a variety of stock indices, as well as commodities, bonds or even a basket of assets. Although similar to mutual funds in many ways, ETF shares trade like common stock on an exchange. The price will change throughout the day as shares are bought and sold, without turnover costs or the tax consequences of trading common shares.

Exchange-Traded Funds (ETFs) are one of the fastest growing investment vehicles in the investment industry.

According to ETF.com, more than 260 ETFs launched since January 1, 2018, and there are 1,800 ETFs available in the marketplace. More than $1 trillion is now invested in ETFs, with fresh inflow of $315.4 billion in 2018.

How Mutual Funds Work

A mutual fund is simply an investment company with a specific investment objective. Thousands of investors with a particular investment objective pool their money into a common account which is then employed by the fund's money manager to achieve that objective.

An investment objective is the fundamental reason you are investing. An investment objective can also define how a mutual fund invests its portfolio. For example, regarding mutual funds, the stated investment objective indicates a particular fund's investment goals, based on the wording in a fund's prospectus.[6]

Here are the parts and pieces it takes to make that happen:

Investment Advisor: This is the professional money manager, usually a money management firm, that makes the investment decisions to achieve the investment objective of the fund. The Advisor sometimes delegates the money management function to a selected Sub-Advisor.

The Administration Firm: This is the firm, usually independent from the fund, that tracks the investors (shareholders), calculates the daily net asset value (total value of the fund divided by the number of shares outstanding), and assesses and accrues the daily cost of operating the fund. It also generally handles the fund registration with the SEC and various states, generally prepares the annual and semi-annual reports to shareholders, calculates and pays share dividends, etc.

The Underwriter/Distributor: This firm is responsible for marketing the fund through brokers and/or directly to shareholders, paying broker commissions, developing marketing material, etc.

The Custodial Bank: Numerous large commercial banks offer custodial services. The bank sets up a segregated account for each mutual fund for which they serve in this capacity. They hold all money and securities for the fund and report the amounts daily to both the Investment Advisor and the Administration Firm.

Fund Counsel: This is a law firm with expertise pertaining to the Securities and Exchange Commission (1940 Act). The firm oversees the fund complex from a compliance perspective to make sure the fund continues to operate within regulatory requirements.

Fund Auditors: This is usually a CPA firm that specializes in mutual fund auditing. They audit every fund in the fund family and issue their audit opinion annually.

How to Invest in a Mutual Fund

Suppose you want to invest in the fund of your choice:

a. You send your check (payable to the fund) to the Administration Firm.

b. They deposit the money in the Custodial Bank account and record your purchase of fund shares at that night's share value which they calculate, after the markets close, every night by summing the market value of all securities and cash held less the daily expense accrual. Then, they divide this sum by the number of shares outstanding. The next day, in most cases, they send you a confirmation of your purchase.

c. The Investment Advisor (or Sub-Advisor) is notified of all new cash infusions and chooses when and where to invest the money.

d. The number of shares you purchased will not change, however, the daily value will fluctuate as a result of the daily change in the market price of the underlying securities owned by the fund.

How to Invest in an Exchange-Traded Fund

An ETF is bought and sold in the marketplace just like a stock, which is where the name "exchange traded" originates. There are two primary ways in which a person may purchase an ETF:

a. A self-directed investment account such as an investment account with an electronic trading platform or a bank's on-line stock trading program.

b. With the help of a licensed investment advisor, registered

representative or certified financial planner. Most common-
ly referred to as a financial advisor, any person who holds a
CFP designation or the Series 7 or 65 license may assist you
in the purchase of an ETF.

Timothy Plan Basics

Timothy Plan is a family of mutual funds, the owner of which
are the shareholders. Timothy Partners, Ltd. is the engine behind
Timothy Plan, making it available to individuals who desire to have
biblically responsible portfolios. It is also the organization that
oversees the investments.

Timothy Partners is the distributor and advisor of the mutual
funds and is responsible for making them available through brokers. As advisor, it is responsible for making sure they are biblically
sound and competitive in the marketplace.

Timothy Plan ETFs are distributed by Foreside Fund Services,
Inc., with Timothy Partners providing the same biblical oversight
as provided for the mutual funds.

The Opportunity to Make a Difference

Nearly $16 trillion is invested in mutual funds,[7] and about 68
percent is held by Christians, as well as 41 percent of all money
invested in securities.[8]

Many activist movements represent a tiny fraction of the population. With less than 1% of our population effecting change within
our nation, imagine the possible impact of Christians investing with
a purpose beyond financial return.

Christians in America have been blessed beyond measure to be living in a self-governing, prosperous nation in which we're free to worship according to our conscience and to practice our faith.

It's not unreasonable to allocate our resources, including our time and finances, in ways bringing glory to God and encouraging biblical values in our culture.

Simply stated, we need to put our money where it complements our faith. In God's economy, we must consider not only investments that bring a healthy return but also what our money is actually doing.

Most people don't have the time or expertise to sort out the market, which is why trusted Christian financial advisors are so important.

In a sermon about the proper uses of money, John Wesley said this:

"I. We ought to gain all we can gain but this it is certain we ought not to do; we ought not to gain money at the expense of life, nor at the expense of our health.

II. Do not throw the precious talent into the sea.

III. Having, first, gained all you can, and, secondly saved all you can, then 'give all you can.'"[9]

Now we can earn returns without being invested in things that operate contrary to the love and mission of Christ. With the options available today, and the knowledge of those options, you're either working with God or against Him. God enables us to allocate his resources, and therefore it is our responsibility to ensure the allocation is honorable to God.

As the mutual fund industry grew, a new phenomenon—socially responsible investing—began taking hold, as activists tried to steer investing toward aiding mainly social causes, such as environmentalism.

Sometimes, this had significant impact, as in generating worldwide pressure forcing an end to South Africa's apartheid regime.

So, why not use a biblically responsible mutual fund to steer money away from companies promoting sin and disparaging God's kingdom values, and toward companies that don't aid cultural corrosion?

It was time to create a vehicle to do just that—which brings us to Timothy Plan's founding, after some fascinating family history.

> If you're not a part of this great movement that is quietly making an impact on the Kingdom, there's no reason why you can't join. It doesn't take a lot of money, only a commitment to ensure our investments are being managed consistently with our values and convictions. Ask your financial advisor to consider your faith when selecting investment options.

[1] Aaron Leavitt, "A Brief History of Mutual Funds," MutualFunds.com, Sept. 2, 2014, at mutualfunds.com/education/mutual-funds-brief-history.
[2] Ibid.
[3] James McWhinney, "A Brief History of the Mutual Fund," Investopedia, Feb. 6, 2018, at investopedia.com/articles/mutualfund/05/mfhistory.asp.
[4] Ibid.
[5] Ibid.
[6] Kent Thune, "Investment Objectives," The Balance, Apr. 1, 2019, at thebalance.com/invest-objective-definition-and-examples-2466572.
[7] 2015 Investment Company Fact Book, 55th Edition, Investment Company Institute, Washington, D.C. (ici.org)
[8] 2014 Religious Landscape Study, conducted June 4-Sept. 30, 2014. Pew Research Center (pewforum.org).
[9] John Wesley, "The Use of Money," Sermon 50, John Wesley Sermons, the United Methodist Church, 1872 (The text for John Wesley's sermons originally came from the Christian Classics Ethereal Library) at umcmission.org/Find-Resources/John-Wesley-Sermons/Sermon-50-The-Use-of-Money.

6

From Migrant's Son to BRI Pioneer

"For I know the plans I have for you," declares the Lord, "plans to prosper you and not to harm you, plans to give you hope and a future"—Jeremiah 29:11

Each of us has a history that influences who we are and what path we take. For Art Ally, it was a grandfather with vision and a father who persevered. He grew up in a culture of gratitude for the opportunities found in America. His father modeled American midwestern values to his children. It is evident in Art's journey that God clearly had a plan for him. He has a plan for all of us. Invested with Purpose requires us to take risks and move out of our comfort zone. We may have to make sacrifices in order to embrace what God has for us in the future.

Art Ally's father ("Art, Sr.") was an immigrant born in Liftaya in the district of Homs, the third largest population area in the Syrian Arab Republic.

Located about 100 miles northwest of Damascus, Homs has a rich history. Its ancient cities were subject to several conquerors, from the Romans to the Ottomans. The Bible documents that Solomon captured it and built several cities there (2 Chronicles 8:3-6)[1].

The family left Liftaya and moved to Jericho before ending up in Lifta, in Palestine, in what is now the greater Jerusalem area of Israel.

As a boy, Art, Sr. tended camels for the family during the Turkish occupation in the early 20th Century. His father, Rashid, seeking to avoid being drafted into the Turkish army during World War I, arranged passage to the United States.

"That was when people were proud to come to America," Art points out. "And become Americans."

Rashid was inducted into the U.S. Army in 1917 and was discharged in 1918. Because of his service, he was granted American citizenship.

After his wife died, he later remarried in America. In 1926, Rashid and his two sons (Ali and Hamuda) set sail from Cherbourg, France, to the United States to live with his American family. On the Ellis Island records, Rashid was listed as being a Semitic Arab from Palestine,

ALI (ART, SR) WITH COUSIN HABIBA, LEFT, AND BROTHER HAMUDA (HENRY). IN LIFTA IN 1920

as were his sons. Art, Sr. (Ali) could not speak or understand English. When he came to America around the age of 15, he was placed in the fourth grade. Easily the oldest in his class, he was humiliated to have to sit at a desk much too small for him.

When his fourth-grade teacher asked him for his name, he responded, "Ali." When she asked for his last name, he repeated, "Ali." The teacher wound up giving him his American name—Arthur Ally ("Art, Sr.").

Art, Sr. had a hard time due to the language barrier, and so he quit school in the sixth grade. Although he was never a practicing Muslim, he believed the only "real" religion came from the Koran, which had been—and still is—the dominant text of the Islamic region where he grew up.

Still dealing with the language barrier and barely having three years of schooling, Art, Sr. managed to find work and even marry his wife Virginia.

He worked for a bakery and made about $15 a month. The struggles they faced and overcame were steep. When Art, Sr. came home on payday, he knew he was in trouble when the heating bill was more than his paycheck. He ended up getting a second job with Berthold & Grigsby (florist shop) as a clerk.

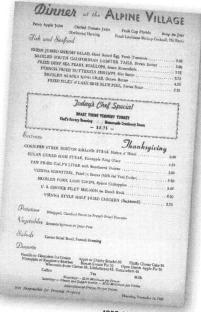

1955 ALPINE VILLAGE THANKSGIVING MENU

His entrepreneurial spirit led him to buy flowers on the side from Berthold Grigsby so his wife could make corsages they sold in front of night clubs.

She had already started her own thriving business growing and selling gladiolas in front of their house, which was on the way to a cemetery. At one point, she had 100,000 gladiolas. As annual flowers, they needed replanting every year.

1975 MAITRE D' ART ALLY BESIDE PRESIDENT FORD AT THE SHERATON-CLEVELAND HOTEL

Meanwhile, Art, Sr.'s hard work and earnest demeanor caught the eye of Herman Pirchner, owner of the Alpine Village, an upscale restaurant in downtown Cleveland. He asked Art if he would work for him as a waiter, and Art answered yes. He strived for excellence and eventually became maître d'hôtel and banquet captain at a restaurant located in the Sheraton-Cleveland Hotel. Through the years, Art, Sr. met several presidents, including Dwight Eisenhower, John Kennedy, Lyndon Johnson, Richard Nixon, and Gerald Ford.

Modest Beginnings

Art Ally was born in 1942, the middle child of five. He was raised by his mom and dad in a three-bedroom home in a western suburb of Cleveland on eight acres of land. The

1956 FAMILY HOME

family had horses, a cow, and chickens. "We lived on eggs," Art said. As a boy, Art helped farm, milk the cow and clean the barn stalls. "I went to school smelling like a cow barn," he explained. One day, his brother was sent to gather eggs, and "was attacked by bandy roosters," Art said. The boys used to ride the horses around and

PICTURED FROM LEFT: TOMMY, DAD, JUDY, MOM, ART

generally raise Cain. They would tear through the barn and grab a pole to dismount.

They played all sorts of games, including baseball. "We created a baseball field on the farm and even built a backstop for it. My older brother picked fights for me with his friends' younger brothers.

"We rode our bicycles all over town without worrying about getting attacked. It was a good, wholesome time and place to grow up.

"I grew up in a great home," Art recalls. "We had strict values: Behave or you're in trouble. Well, I got in a bit of trouble every now and then. My dad worked nights, so we ran a little wild at times. But we'd be home by 6 p.m. for dinner. It was a safe community and had a small-town feel. We

1946: ART ON HIS HORSE BLONDE

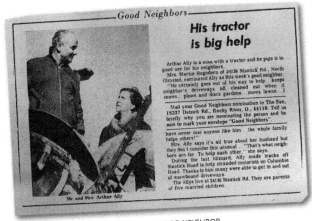

Good Neighbors

His tractor is big help

Arthur Ally is a man with a tractor and he puts it to good use for his neighbors.

Mrs. Martin Hagedorn of 24126 Mastick Rd., North Olmsted, nominated Ally as this week's good neighbor. "He certainly goes out of his way to help ... keeps neighbor's driveways all cleaned out when it snows, plows and discs gardens ... mows lawns ...I

Mail your Good Neighbors nomination to The Sun, 19337 Detroit Rd., Rocky River, O., 44116. Tell us briefly why you are nominating the person and be sure to mark your envelope "Good Neighbors".

have never met anyone like him ... the whole family helps others!"

Mrs. Ally says it's all true about her husband but they don't consider this unusual ... "That's what neighbors are for. To help each other," she says.

During the last blizzard, Ally made tracks off Mastick Road to help stranded motorists on Columbia Road. Thanks to him many were able to get in and out of snowbound driveways.

The Allys live at 24136 Mastick Rd. They are parents of five married children.

Mr. and Mrs. Arthur Ally

1973: ART & VIRGINIA ALLY BEING A GOOD NEIGHBOR

never even locked our doors.

"People had basic values. At that time, the church was respected, not maligned as it is today. However, we still looked at churchgoers as a bunch of hypocrites. They'd go on Sunday, dress up in their Sunday best, but live like hellions the rest of the week. Watching them, we had Mahatma Gandhi's view, who said he'd consider being a Christian—if he ever met one."

Art was like most teenagers, although he did excel in school and had a keen love for mathematics, especially when it came to numbers. He often referred to this as "understanding the nature of numbers in the universe."

He fell in love with his wife Bonnie in high school. They were married in 1961, and have three children—Douglas, Stephen and Cheryl—and as of 2019, 10 grandchildren and 11 great-grandchildren.

One of the most amazing experiences in Art's life was when he and his older brother Ted joined forces in 1979 to take their father Art, Sr. back to the Middle East, and specifically to Palestine (now Israel) after he had been gone for 53 years. He had not been back since leaving with his father for the United States when he was 14. Bonnie and Ted's wife were along, too.

"We arrived at the Tel Aviv airport, and 10 family members were standing there with tears in their eyes—my dad had finally come home. We stayed with his family in Ramallah, where people lined up to see him every day. They had walked miles to see him and his sons. Actually, my older brother received all the attention because he was the first-born."

"Art, Sr., got a lot of attention, too. Our family there focused efforts on finding a new wife for my father, since my mom had died several years prior," Art stated. "But he was still mourning the death of my mom and had no interest in a new wife."

Afterward, Art's Palestinian cousin drove the family all around the Holy Land in a square-back Volkswagen van, and since he was Muslim,

1979 BIRTHPLACE IN LIFTA
PICTURE LEFT TO RIGHT:
ART SR, TED, BONNIE, NANCY

he did not go into the Church of the Sepulchre or other sites where Jesus had been.

"What moved us most was walking where Jesus walked," Art expressed, noting he and Bonnie, for the past ten years, try to visit the Holy Land every two years.

He recalls marveling at what the Israelis did in the Six-Day War in 1967, especially in the Golan Heights. "They had six tanks against 200 Syrian tanks, but miraculously, the Syrians wound up running away. When God says He has His hand on Israel, He means it. How else could Israel exist,

2017 ART & BONNIE IN JERUSALEM

surrounded by enemies and outnumbered 10,000 to one? A guide on one of our tours pointed out with a smile, 'Our enemies keep trying to push us into the sea. What they don't realize is Jews don't swim! Think of Moses parting the Red Sea, Joshua parting the Jordan River, and Jesus walking on water.'"

Bonnie and Art

1960: BONNIE & ART

Bonnie Danielson's mother, Jeanette, grew up on a dairy farm of 180 acres in Frewsburg, New York, near Jamestown. Jeanette met Wilmer, her future husband, during a holiday celebration in New York where he was visiting his uncle.

Bonnie's father had previously worked at the General Motors factory during World War II building submarine engines, where he had lost the majority of his hearing. After an attempt at starting a chicken farm stalled, he worked at Danco, his father's sheet metal shop in Cleveland, until he retired.

Bonnie was born in 1942 and while in the fourth grade her family moved to a home a quarter mile from Art. They attended different elementary schools.

Their paths crossed a few times while growing up but it wasn't until high school when they became good friends. The relationship was anything but romantic at first. In fact, Art used to fix up Bonnie with his friends. "I remember in 1960, shortly after graduation, Art and I went on a double date to Lake Erie. We each had different dates. Art started chasing me, and in an attempt to get away, I splashed him with my Coke. He caught me and tossed me in the lake. It was a turning point for our relationship, we realized we belonged together."

As Art recalls it, "Bonnie threw a Coke at me, and I threw her into the water and nearly drowned her." Apparently, she didn't mind too much, because, "we went home as a couple."

"Art was like James Dean—he had a black leather jacket, a black shirt and tight jeans, and a pompadour haircut," Bonnie beamed. "He was very good looking. However, it seemed as soon as we started dating, he cut off all of his beautiful hair. He came to my door, and when I opened it, his hair was all gone!"

Having registered for the draft, Art went down to the Army recruiting office in an attempt to enlist. After being kept waiting for what he says was a very long time, he got up and left.

Bonnie encouraged Art to start attending the Congregationalist church where she worshiped with her family. Art was curious—he always had been, since his family never went to church.

Looking back, both Art and Bonnie realized it was a very liberal church. Bonnie recalled, "We didn't actually hear the Gospel." When asked about Noah's Ark the pastor told Bonnie the Bible stories were just stories. Ultimately, their first church did not have a significant impact on their lives.

While dating, Art talked his father into giving him his old car after he had bought a new car instead of trading it in. Art, in an attempt to rebuild the engine, turned the family's chicken barn into a garage. Art and several of his high school buddies—who had no idea what they were doing—pulled out the engine, replaced the rings and bearings on the pistons, and put it all back together. The problem was, the "rebuilt engine" wouldn't start. They took it to a real mechanic who corrected the way they had put in the distributor. Although the car started, it only lasted half a day," Art said, "before it blew up."

Low on funds, Art borrowed money from Bonnie to pay for a new engine. "I figured it was probably cheaper to marry her than to pay her back," he said with a dead serious expression yet a twinkle in his eye.

Before their marriage, both of them enrolled in Ohio State, "right down the road in Columbus," but Art eventually quit and tried to find a job to support his soon-to-be wife.

"Back then, I was cocky. I didn't think I needed to go to college. I thought I could simply go to work. I applied all over town for a job, including at a local finance company.

Unbeknownst to Art, until fifty years later when Bonnie finally

1961 ART AND BONNIE'S MATRIMONY

revealed her secret, he learned she was concerned about marrying an unemployed fiancé. She called the finance company and asked if they were going to hire him, because, she told them, 'I'm going to marry him.'" He got the job.

And marry they did, both at age 19, with a reception for 300 people at Bonnie's parents' house. "The ceremony took place in "the little Congregational church where I had grown up," Bonnie said. Art was not yet a believer but wanted to make his new wife happy, so they continued going to church there after they were wed. (For Art's Christian testimony, see Chapter 11.)

When Art and Bonnie bought their first home, it was in a new development, so they were able to purchase it because of a landscape allowance of $2,000 the developer granted if they would do the landscaping themselves. Art figured he was going to really fertilize the yard. He had heard about a sewage processing plant about five miles from their home that gave away dried, processed sewage to anybody who wanted it. "We ordered a truckload of that stuff," Art said. "We were not home when the truck delivered its load and were shocked to find it was anything except dried, processed sewage."

Art figured, since his father owned a full-sized Ford tractor and all the equipment, he would simply borrow it to spread the raw sewage around the yard. "Bottom line: it was a total mess. We finally completed the job and the result was having the best-looking yard in the neighborhood. The problem was every time it rained, the smell came back."

Art and Bonnie both had good role models, with both sets of parents marrying for life. Bonnie's mom put her dream of becoming a nurse on hold to raise her children. She eventually took courses and became a Practical Nurse.

The couple had only a one-day honeymoon—July 4—at Cedar Point amusement park in Sandusky, Ohio. Art was scheduled to start his new job with the finance company the next day.

"We've made up for it since," Art said. "We've been everywhere together—Israel, Singapore, Australia, you name it. We prefer to take the slow route via cruise ships."

Then he was ready to switch gears again.

1991 ABOARD ONE OF THE COUNTLESS CRUISES

We need to revisit what has shaped us to be who we are today, and who sacrificed to get us there. Do you know what God's plan for you is? If we don't know where we've been, we won't know where we're going. Those who are Invested with Purpose have a keen sense of history though they are not imprisoned by it. It inspires them to move forward, informs their convictions, and gives them grit. We can know with certainty that God has a plan for us even though we may not always know what it is.

[1] "Then Solomon went to Hamath-zobah and captured it. He built Tadmor in the wilderness, along with all the store cities that he had built in Hamath." Hamath-zobah is in Homs.

7

The Early Years

For we are God's handiwork, created in Christ Jesus to do good works, which God prepared in advance for us to do.—Ephesians 2:10

Being Invested with Purpose requires preparation. We won't find purpose on Day One, yet we must persist and learn all we can, trusting the Lord will guide us. We may not even know what we're looking for, but God knows where He is taking us. He will prepare us through formal education, experience, and disappointments. Preparation is vital; without it, we cannot rise to excellence.

After three years with the finance company, Art rose to the position of assistant manager. The company announced they were opening six new branches in Texas and offered Art the one in Sherman.

In the mid-Sixties, the Ally family packed up and moved to Texas, where Art did his best to settle into the local culture, which, as it turned out, wasn't so hard. "I became a Texan," he said with a laugh. "I talked like 'em. Thought like 'em. After three years, we realized we had no future there, so we moved back to Cleveland."

Because of Art's background in credit and finance, he was able to get a job as a credit manager in a Montgomery Ward store. After a couple of years in that position, he concluded there was not a bright future there either. He resigned and along with their two children, Doug and Steve, they moved into the basement of Bonnie's parents' house. He enrolled at Cleveland State University night school to finally earn a college degree. Meanwhile, Bonnie, who had earned a license in cosmetology, brought in income from her vocation.

Ally Will Head Finance Company

Arthur Ally has been named manager of the new Civic Finance Company which opens officially Monday, April 12, at 222 South Travis Street in Sherman.

Civic Finance is the Texas subsidiary of the Capital Finance Corporation. Capital is an 18-state organization with headquarters in Columbus, Ohio. It operates more than 300 offices.

Ally joined Capital in July, 1961, as a branch representative for the East Ninth Street office in Cleveland, Ohio. He was transferred to the branch in Fairview, Ohio in March 1962, and was made assistant manager in April, 1963. In April, 1964, he was assigned to the branch office in Parma, Ohio.

Ally was born in North Olmsted, Ohio, and was graduated from the North Olmsted H i g h School. He attended Ohio State University. He and his wife, Bonnie, have two children. They will make their home in Sherman at 645 Denton Drive.

With his background in collections and credit, he started his own credit collection company to earn a living while going to night school. He accelerated his courses and received a four-year degree—accounting with an economics minor—in two

1969: ART, BONNIE, STEVE & DOUG

and a half years. Following graduation, he was accredited as a Certified Public Accountant on August 9, 1974.

Since their heart was still in Texas, they decided to move back.

"My whole goal upon earning my bachelor's degree at CSU was to obtain a law degree from the University of Texas, which offered a night school option to their law school," Art said.

"We left the kids with Bonnie's parents and drove to Austin, where we learned they recently disbanded the night school portion of their law school. We decided to head to Dallas, where I thought I could find a job. The one thing I knew for sure was that we did not want to live in Houston. However, as we started the journey from Austin to Dallas, somehow, the car turned onto the freeway toward Houston.

"Upon arriving in Houston, I immediately bought a copy of the Houston Chronicle. In the "help wanted" section of the paper, I found an employment agency called M. David Lowe, which had a lot of ads.

"We checked into a motel. I called M. David Lowe and told them I had just arrived in town,

1975: BONNIE, ART, STEVE, CHERYL & DOUG

had a degree in accounting, and needed a job. Although hesitant, they agreed to see me, so I went right into their office in my travel clothes. They took one look at me and knew I was nuts. I told them, 'look'—I was still a little cocky at the time—'you get me an interview, I will get the job.' They shook their heads and said, 'We'll try.' They called me the next morning with two interview opportunities—one with Browning Ferris and the other with Gulf Oil. As it ended up, both offered me a job. We moved to Houston, bought a house, and I worked for four years for Gulf in their internal audit division."

"Where Do You Want to Live?"

"In search of a career path with the company, I worked on audits in nearly every division of Gulf Oil, but nothing interested me, so I resigned. Then, I started a job for a family-owned business, Texas Pipe and Supply, as Controller. I stayed there for three years, but totally lost interest in accounting. I really wanted to enter either the computer industry or become a stockbroker. I checked ads in Houston. Bache Halsey Stuart Shields was hiring; after extensive testing and several interviews, they offered me a job in their training program to become a registered financial advisor in their Houston branch. That's when I really took a chance, thanked them for the offer and told them we really didn't want to live in Houston anymore. Well, that shocked them. So, they asked me, 'where do you want to live?'

"Since Bonnie's parents had moved to Orlando, I responded that we would like to live in Orlando. As fate would have it, the company recruiter who offered me the Houston job happened to be good friends with the Bache manager in Orlando.

"He called him and asked if he had any openings, and he did. Initially, I flew to Orlando, where I interviewed and was offered a job. I returned with my daughter Cheryl and lived at my in-laws, while Bonnie and the boys stayed back to pack up the house.

"I was a bit like a fish out of water, though, because their training program was geared to create stockbrokers, which didn't interest me at all by then. My passion was to be a financial planner for my clients,

1978: ART ALLY AT BACHE - WINTER PARK, FLORIDA

something unheard of at that time in the industry. As a result, I struggled through my first year. Then things fell into place. I actually became their top-producing broker in the branch by being a financial planner instead of a stockbroker. From the beginning, my goal was to become a branch manager. I went through their management training program and ended up at an existing branch in Lexington, Kentucky, which needed a manager. We moved to Lexington.

"Things were going fine until E.F. Hutton moved into town and began recruiting my top reps. They offered enticing bonuses to my brokers if they would move their book of business to E.F. Hutton. Well, management assumes it's the manager's fault when brokers leave, so they fired me."

Returning to Florida

"We came back to Orlando, where I had my original clients. I joined a different firm, the Winter Park branch of Shearson-Lehman/American Express, in 1983. I had to

1983: ART ALLY AT SHEARSON BROTHERS - WINTER PARK, FLORIDA

start rebuilding a book of business from scratch, since I had given away all my clients when I went into management with the exception of a couple of clients that I brought with me.

"The following year they asked me to manage the Ormond Beach branch, and I worked there for three years. Meanwhile, I studied to become a Certified Financial Planner. Then, a problem arose in the Boca Raton office, and they asked me to manage it. I was reluctant because our daughter was a sophomore in high school and had already moved five times during her schooling. We chose to go down there anyway and it was beautiful. I was the token Christian in a branch full of Jewish brokers."

A Family Stranded

One thing you could count on, Art loved to take cruises. The cruise of 1987 was different from the others. It was the summer before Cheryl's senior year. Art, Bonnie, Steve and Cheryl sailed the Caribbean during Regent Star's inaugural year. Cheryl recalled,

"Staff wore white gloves and served flaming baked Alaska."

All was well until something unexpected happened. The ship caught on fire in the galley kitchen causing the loss of power and plumbing for several hours. Eventually we made it to the port in Jamaica a day early.

Jamaica was not prepared for this. Passengers took taxis to multiple locations on the island. Since the passengers flights were not scheduled until the following day, it made things quite challenging.

The Allys, along with a few hundred other guests, were taken to a place with a pool and outside bar. People were hot, cranky, very hungry and the food was not being served. Art and Bonnie saw the panic in the servers' faces so they rolled up their sleeves and started helping the staff make hamburgers, french fries and egg sandwiches.

This act of kindness impacted Art and Bonnie's children, that their parents would serve unselfishly despite disrespectful guests yelling at them to hurry it up.

Navigating the Crash

Art was the manager of the Boca branch when the stock market crashed to 1,738.74 on October 19, 1987, losing nearly 1,000 points from its high the summer before. He told the Boca Raton News: "We've just seen a year's worth of movement corrected in one day. It makes no sense; it's purely emotional, a real panic!"

The News continued: "Earlier, when volume hit 300 million shares, Ally said that traders were worried whether the market's computers could handle 500 million orders, as the tape ran more than an hour behind the heavy trading. It had never been tested beyond 412 million shares. 'I think we're close to the bottom,' Ally said. 'I definitely would not be selling now. On a value basis, there are some great buys today.'"

Once again, we were called to move back to Orlando.

"Doug, our oldest, was in the Navy by then, Steve was off at the University of Kentucky, but we did not move before Cheryl was able to graduate from Spanish River High School in Boca Raton.

"Every move we made was tough on the kids. We had lots of family talks. We would tell them, 'love where you live.'"

From Big Firm to Independence

In 1990, Art ran for the state legislature, losing by only six votes.

"After that, Shearson, for whom I still worked, made a new policy forbidding any employee from running for public office, so I resigned. I looked around and found office space right across the street from Shearson.

"I learned Raymond James Financial had a boutique division called Investment Management & Research (IM&R). I decided to open a branch, which we named Covenant Financial Management ("Covenant) with IM&R as the Broker/Dealer. That's when I learned a big lesson. The big firms say you get your clients because of them, but I found my clients stayed with me in spite of Shearson, not because of it."

SUN Politics

THE SUN Thursday, August 23, 1990 Page 24

Maitland financial planner Ally joins District 34 race

By SHERI FOX SAVAS
Sun Staff Writer

Maitland resident Art Ally said he is challenging incumbent state Representative Frank Stone (R-Casselberry) for the District 34 seat because he wants to bring common sense, values and financial acumen to state government.

"I am running not of a just for political office but out of conviction," Ally said. "I just don't like what is happening in Florida and America.

Ally, 48, said his campaign platform is three-pronged.

First, the Republican candidate said he wants to reduce the size of government in order to make it more accountable to the people and to eliminate waste.

Second, Ally said he wants to end the trampling of individuals' rights, including property rights and parental rights.

Third, Ally said he wants to see morals and values put back into government, education, the courts and the media.

Ally, who has worked as a certified financial planner for 12 years and a certified public accountant for 15 years, said his financial background makes him particularly able to serve Florida's needs.

"As a professional financial planner who serves his clients by successfully blending their goals and objectives with financial assets and liabilities, I would like to help the state of Florida build a sounder financial base of operation in order to better serve

the needs of Florida citizens without raising taxes," he said.

In education, Ally said he is opposed to establishment of progressive promotion, a system by which students in kindergarten through fifth grade are automatically promoted to the next grade.

The candidate said if elected, he would work to reduce Department of Education bureaucracy and reallocate the money saved to the classroom.

Ally graduated Magna Cum Laude from Cleveland State University with a B.A. in business administration.

He has worked as vice-president and financial consultant with Shearson, Lehman Brothers for seven years.

Ally is a member of the Central Florida Estate Planning Council, the Planned Giving Council of Central Florida, the Florida Institute of Certified Public Accountants, the International Association of Financial Planning, and the Who's Who of American Finance.

His community work includes membership on the Florida Hospital Giving Committee and the Orlando Regional Medical Center Planned Giving Advisory Council.

He worked as chairman of the United Way's Planned Giving Committee for South Palm Beach County and Ormond Beach for five years.

Ally is president of the Christian Action Council of Central Florida and a member of the board of directors for both the

Liberty Council and the Christian Coalition of Florida.

He is also a member of the Winter Park Rotary Club, the Central Florida Right to Life and the First Baptist Church of Winter Park.

Ally lives in Maitland with his wife, Bonnie. They have three children: Douglas, 28; Stephen, 26 and Cheryl, 20 and three grandchildren: Gregory, 5; Heather, 3; Jeffrey, 2.

Steve joined his Dad at Covenant and began studying for a Series 7 securities license.

An Opportunity Wrapped in a Problem

One day, Art had a fateful lunch with a Christian friend, who told him, "Art, what you need under Covenant is a specialty." He was an officer at the Christian Management Association, and he told Art that pastors of independent churches had no retirement plans and something needed to be done.

"This really appealed to me, so I started looking into mutual funds and annuity companies and began developing a retirement plan package," Art said. "But then, I found out, I could not in good conscience do it. Pastors were in the pulpit preaching against abortion and pornography. Except, we would be investing their money in companies involved in it. I looked around for a 'clean' investment alternative but found nothing.

"That's when I learned to talk to Bonnie before making any business decisions. I mean really talk to her. I have scars from all the times I didn't. She said, 'We have to start one,' meaning create a financial product for pastors that would not violate biblical values."

Bonnie got excited and went through a number of our biblical-

1990 ART AND BONNIE START THEIR NEW ADVENTURE

ly based financial study materials, which is where she came up with the Bible verses that are Timothy Plan's founding references:

> But if anyone does not provide for his own, and especially for those of his household, he has denied the faith and is worse than an unbeliever.— 1 Timothy 5:8

> Do not lay hands suddenly on anyone, and do not partake of other men's sins. Keep yourself pure.— 1 Timothy 5:22

Enter Steve and Cheryl

"When my Dad started Timothy Partners, Ltd., to be the distributor of the Timothy Plan mutual fund, I studied for and obtained a Series 24 license. I became a registered principal to manage Covenant Financial Management while Art was in the throes of starting this crazy idea of Timothy Plan," Steve said.

"We wanted to keep Covenant open using IM&R—Raymond James agreed—but they preferred to ease Art out of the branch (since he was creating a separate mutual fund). I replaced my father as branch manager.

"Then, once Timothy Plan launched, Art decided he really needed me to be part of the team. We sold Covenant's book of business and I joined the firm."

At the time, Cheryl was working towards her degree in Elementary Education. "She came to Covenant to help with our office, temporarily (or so she thought)," Art said.

"That is when I came to fully understand the real meaning of R&D (research and development). It really means all outgo and no income. Despite this fact, Bonnie left her administrative position at the church to work with me.

"When Cheryl first joined our team," Art said, "I got mad because she was always playing on her computer with artsy-craftsy stuff. It finally dawned on me she is a self-taught artist with a lot of talent."

She's now putting those skills and talent to work as Chief Marketing Officer, managing the company branding and coordinating the design of the website and publications.

> How has God equipped you for the purpose He has in store for you? How is He preparing you now? Identify areas in which you must still learn and grow to realize the vision He has placed in your heart. As Biblical Entrepreneurship founder Patrice Tsague states, "Opportunity is where preparation meets God's timing."

A Nehemiah Plan for an Election

ART ONCE RAN FOR PUBLIC OFFICE WHILE STILL WORKING FOR SHEARSON.

"Having been involved in Central Florida's pro-life movement, a group of us got really concerned about our very liberal Republican state representative, who was running unopposed for his fourth term," Art said. "We sat around pointing fingers at each other that someone had to oppose this guy. And nobody had the time, inclination or desire to do it. The day before the filing deadline, he was still unopposed.

"They pointed at me, and I said, 'all right, but I've never done this, I have no desire to do it, but I will go file.' We drove up to Tallahassee and filed, and I got on the ballot. We had six weeks before the primary to mount a campaign. None of us had any idea what we were doing. But we did come up with a biblical plan based on the principles in the Book of Nehemiah—where Nehemiah was faced with a seemingly insurmountable job of rebuilding the totally devastated wall around Jerusalem while surrounded by his enemies.

ART ALLY
FOR
STATE REPRESENTATIVE

BACK TO THE BASICS
FOR A STRONGER FUTURE

REPUBLICAN DISTRICT 34

"From man's perspective, it was impossible. But God gave him a plan. And that was to assign every family a section of the wall. They were not to look to the left or the right but only to their own section. By doing it this way, this impossible task was completed in 52 days, with people who had a sword in one hand and a brick in the other.

"So we decided to implement that strategy in this campaign. The idea was to locate a solid Christian in every precinct in our district who would be concerned only with their precinct, i.e., their neighborhood. God raised up 150 Christians to help with the campaign, none of whom had ever worked on a campaign before. We had probably 140 or so precincts in Seminole County, about 40 in Brevard County and one precinct in Orange County.

"As amateurs, we were only able to raise $13,000 for this campaign while the incumbent had a war chest of $400,000 for his re-election. We had only enough to pay for yard signs and one brochure for the volunteers to hand out in their precinct. Due to our time restrictions, we really only focused on Seminole County, where all of our volunteers were. I did manage to make two trips to Brevard County to knock on a few doors. I didn't even know where the Orange County precinct was."

"My Dad filed way late and ran against an incumbent," Steve

recalled. "Those were hard days. We canvassed precincts. I was walkin' and knockin'."

They hit every precinct in Seminole County. "But we never got to the little hamlet of Christmas, tucked into a corner near the Seminole Ranch Wildlife Management Area, and about halfway between Orlando and Cape Canaveral," Steve said.

"When Art ran for state legislator, he and I drove around the day of the election and met people and shook hands," Terry Covert said. "We had thought of going to the precinct over in Orange County, but decided we had better stay around here."

"On Election night, Seminole County reported first, and the Orlando Sentinel declared me the victor," Art said. "My opponent lived in Brevard County. So, when their results came in, my commanding lead shrank to a 13-vote lead. Then, the lone precinct in Orange County, which I never visited but my opponent worked, reported. And I lost the election by six votes. I had to live that down for the next two years because that lone Orange County precinct contained the town of Christmas, so I became known as 'the Christian who forgot Christmas.'

"The end result of that was—God is in control; He knows what He's doing. Had I won that election, I would have sat in the sessions and been patted on the head and ignored for my strong Christian beliefs, and I never would have started Timothy Plan. So, He knows what He is doing. Timothy Plan has had a thousand times more impact on the Kingdom than my sitting there getting pats on the head."

The Passion Behind Biblically Responsible Investing

Without faith it is impossible to please God
—Hebrews 11:6

> Investing with Purpose requires passion, and pursuing passion requires faith. Faith is essential to please God. Art had lots of passion, and through his faith, he persevered until he succeeded.

In 2018, Art's daughter Cheryl penned an article, "Why Art Ally Is Not THE Expert on Biblically Responsible Investing." She briefly traced family history, and offered some thoughts about why Timothy Plan was an idea whose time had come:

"One thing you could count on is my dad never settled for mediocrity. He always looked ahead to see how he could improve his knowledge—and his family's income. But it came at a cost—way too many moves and financial roles," Cheryl remembers. "Since I was pretty much the only child at this point, I experienced all of the pro-life rallies and events my parents dragged me to. I honestly had no idea how awful abortion was. He cared for the unborn and was hoping it would impact me in some way.

"My father was like most men during the '70s and '80s. Sunday afternoons he would be relaxing in his recliner, watching football on television with a cold beer in his hand. In addition to being the master of making homemade vanilla ice cream, he perfected the art of piña coladas. Those are fond memories for me.

"During my senior year, the night before my prom, something tragic happened. A call came in the middle of the night. My brother Steve was in a horrible accident involving alcohol, totaling his new white Mustang, near the west coast. He had broken his neck, was in a hospital, and required a halo brace to be screwed into his skull. My parents drove for hours to get to the hospital. It was at that moment my father banished any forms of alcohol in his home. He wanted to be a good example to those around him. This is what partly led him to be so passionate about the screens we use today."

There are so many stories to tell about the trials, blessings, and miracles experienced by launching a Christian mutual fund, giving Christians an alternative to worldly investing. The term "Biblically Responsible Investing" didn't exist at that time. It was often called "Values-Based Investing," "Morally Responsible Investing," "Biblically-Based Investing," and "Faith-Based Investing."

It wasn't until December of 1997 when Art Ally and Mark Minnella of Integrity Investors co-launched the National Association of Christian Financial Consultants—with the passion of Dan Hardt of Dan Hardt Financial Services—that Biblically Responsible Investing stuck. The new association gave Christian advisors a forum to come together, worship, and figure out how to change investors' ideas about investing.

A Good Steward

Over the years, Art took risks. He moved his family all over the U.S., reaching higher at every turn without compromising his convictions.

In 1992, at the age of 52, he risked everything. When he and Bonnie decided to move in faith, sell their house, sell his financial practice, and start the first biblically responsible mutual fund, it was an uncertain time. But that is the definition of faith. And without faith, it is impossible to please God.

Fast forward to 2004, during Timothy Plan's struggles, he felt called to take a leave and write a guide for people to truly understand what God says about money. He ended up authoring the Biblical Stewardship Series utilizing material from Randy Alcorn, Howard Dayton, and others. He was so passionate about this that he sold the six-book series at cost after extensively training advisors to teach it to others. Today, the series, which is made available at no charge on biblicalstewardship.org, is impacting the lives of persons all across the nation and around the world, including home-schoolers in hopes of transforming the next generation.

The Power of a "Rifter"

Dave Hart, who now runs eVALUEator but has worked with Art since 1999 in some capacity, explains the magic behind Art's entrepreneurial success:

"Art is a rifter," Dave says. "Walt Disney was a rifter—someone who finds a rift or gap in the status quo of business life and bets every-thing he has on it. Typically, they are very focused, driven people."

"A financial advisor walked into our office one day and asked, 'Is Art as dogmatic-focused as he was in the beginning when he start-ed this thing?' I said, 'Yes, he is.' He said, 'Good, because I wasn't ready to hear it at that point, but I'm ready to hear it now.'"

Art wanted to open up a retirement plan for non-denominational churches because the Southern Baptists had one, the Methodists had one, the Presbyterians had one, the Catholics had dioceses, these peo-ple all had them, but non-denominational churches had nothing.

Pastors can be so driven that they work their whole lives, giving away most of their money and wind up with nothing. They gen-erally don't retire because they can't, since they have nothing to retire on. Art felt pastors needed some type of retirement fund. He started putting one to-gether and discovered, ev-ery time, the available investment products were involved in some-thing he could not ask a pastor to invest in.

As a result, Art took leave from his business and started looking at company activities, leaving Steve to hold the financial planning business together. Art spent two years developing a solution and soon realized the best option would be to start a mutual fund. This involved finding willing investors to help fund the launch of a mu-tual fund. Cheryl recalls Art saying many times, "if he had any idea what he was going to go through to launch a mutual fund, he might never have done it."

It's interesting that a man of Palestinian descent would be used by God to build a Christian mutual fund and be a strong supporter of Israel.

"Historically, Palestinians tend to hold firm convictions," Steve said. "And that's the kind of person it would take to do what we do. Art acts on what he feels God is telling him to do. Over the years, I have watched him grow from a Sunday churchgoing Christian to a man of great faith."

From here, we will let Art tell his own story how Timothy Plan began.

What are you passionate about? How can you, by faith, transform that passion into making a difference for your community? Remember, without faith, it is impossible to please God.

9

"Obedience Trumps Performance"

...to obey is better than sacrifice—I Samuel 15:22b

> Investing with Purpose requires complete obedience, not partial obedience. No one ever made a real difference without giving themselves entirely to their convictions and following through to the end no matter the cost. Art relates how God steered him toward his calling.

In 1992, I had a successful practice going in Orlando (Covenant Financial Management), and an 18-year career as a financial consultant/branch manager, but I felt called by God to make another change. I was very active in the pro-life community and wanted to do much more for God's kingdom.

My hot button was, while pastors in denominations often had decent retirement plans, the pastors from independent churches were left high and dry. I began to put together a retirement program geared to helping them on a national scale.

I soon realized I could not use companies advocating sin when these pastors were preaching against the evils of abortion and pornography. I looked around for investment products to build biblically responsible portfolios, not only for pastors but also for other Christian investors as well. I could not find an investment that reflected biblical principles. After examining a few socially screened funds and faith-based funds—which excluded companies involved in alcohol and tobacco—none screened for issues such as abortion and pornography.

I had been selling mutual funds for 18 years, but never operated one. I found out early who was the real Chairman of the Board, and it wasn't me. Needing to raise $1 million in capital to get the fund going, I formed Timothy Partners, Ltd. (Timothy Plan's distributor) and made a list of 50 well-to-do friends who could each contribute $50,000 without really missing it. This meant I only needed to find 20 willing people. However, only three actually agreed to invest.

I realized, I only thought I knew who should have been in our partnership group, but God knew all along who He wanted to be part of this. Over the next six months, I met people I had never known before who became initial investors, and we raised the full million dollars.

After two years of research and development, in March 1994, we launched Timothy Plan, a mutual fund based on a founding commitment that we would never compromise biblical principles. We have been faithful throughout, and I believe that's why God has allowed us to proceed and grow.

"Not a Penny"

Our arrival was not met with universal enthusiasm. "This fund may have gone too far. It sounds like someone trying to preach to the converted and then setting up a big collection," mutual fund analyst Michael Lipper told Bloomberg News.[1]

My Wall Street friends all cautioned me what I was about to do was impossible. "You can't do that, you can't exclude investing in some of the most profitable companies and expect to get good returns," they'd say. My answer to them was in God's economy, "obedience trumps performance every time."

Besides, you don't even have to sacrifice performance. At times, we trail, and we're at a comparative disadvantage when the stocks we screen out run wild. But over time, it evens out and we're competitive in the long run.

The original Timothy Plan board of trustees consisted of, top left, Dr. J.C. Mitchell (Treasurer), Gregory F. Tighe (Executive Vice President/Secretary), Mark Schweizer (Trustee), Wesley W. Pennington (Trustee), and myself as President. Over the years, we have expanded into a twelve member board of highly respected leaders in the national Christian community.

Timothy Plan initially focused on five core factors: abortion, pornography, alcohol, tobacco, and casino gambling. Later, we added screens for anti-family entertainment, unbiblical lifestyles, and human rights to the mix. Our screens of gambling, tobacco, and alcohol may be areas where an element of "Christian liberty" could be expressed, but because of the overwhelming abuses and destruction caused to families and society, we screen them.

Our first marketing piece concealed a penny with the following question: "How much money is OK to have invested in abortion or pornography? The answer is simple. Not a penny."

In 1995, eVALUEator was launched, a screening service for advisors identifying companies and mutual funds that own companies actively involved in, profiting from, or financially supporting any one of our screens. Our screening includes eight categories with several sub-categories. For example, our abortion screen consists of sub-screened categories such as abortifacients, cloning, fetal stem-cell research, and donations to organizations like Planned Parenthood.

Early Struggles

Business was slow at first. We began by losing $40,000 to $50,000 each month, despite our materials and operations being of a quality that would rival some of the top firms in the industry. In our first 18 months, we ran out of money. It was the lowest point of my life. All these partners had trusted me with $1 million, and it was gone. I went back to a few of the partners who agreed to inject some more

1996: ART ALLY LOOKING OVER NEW BROCHURE DESIGN

money into the operation, and it carried us for a little while, but growth was still painfully slow. We frankly had difficulty attracting shareholders because of the typical Christian view that business is business and church is church. Over the next five years, we ran out of money four times.

I asked God, "Why aren't people investing with us?" and got a clear answer: Because they don't know and are not being taught. I looked around for resources to share, but there was nothing that pulled it all together.

I told my wife Bonnie I was going to write a course and guidebook on comprehensive biblical stewardship. I asked Randy Alcorn to help with writing, and he was too busy writing his new book. But he did give us permission to use his excellent material, as did Howard Dayton founder of Crown Financial Ministries and Compass. I hibernated in my bedroom office at home and concentrated on the writing.

It took three months to assemble what became the "Biblical Stewardship Series: God's Plan for Financial Success," first published in 2004

ART ALLY HOLDING THE BIBLICAL STEWARDSHIP SERIES

with insight and assistance of finance planning professionals Dan Hardt, Mark Henry, Todd Sadowski, Paul Saxton, Charles Schultz, and others. Mat Staver of Liberty Counsel contributed the chapter on Cultural Stewardship. We recently put together a family edition study guide.

Over the years, the going was rough, yet every time we were in trouble, God led me to people He wanted to be part of our mission.

The last time we were out of money, it was New Year's Eve in 2002. We had a 4 p.m. deadline to come up with the cash or be put out of business by the Securities and Exchange Commission—we just made it.

At one point, realizing we needed to attract more assets from financial advisors, we launched what is known as Class B shares, which pay an upfront sales commission of 4% of the amount that financial advisors invest for their clients in our funds. We learned Class B funds generally do not finance this themselves; they do it through banks and credit lines. I went on a mission to find a Central Florida bank that would grant us a credit line of $1 million to finance these Class B shares, which was a pretty audacious thing to do.

After striking out time after time, I finally found a loan officer who would listen. As I described how this would work, he filled up a legal pad with notes. He then shook his head and explained most of the loans from this bank involved rock-solid real estate deals. We, on the other hand, had no history, and the company behind the new venture was losing money. However, he agreed to present the proposal to the loan committee. He called me back the next day and said, "you're not going to believe this, they approved it!"

"Let Me Get This Straight— You Want to Do What?"

As we expanded with additional funds, we needed additional money managers and went to the institutional division of a respected Broker/Dealer to make our case.

The fellow we spoke to said, "Let me get this straight: You want to do what? You have no money, you're starting with some major stocks excluded, and your fee schedule is less than these money managers offered their largest clients, and you want them to come aboard Timothy Plan?" Yes, we did. And, they did. These consultants turned out to be Christians and even worked for free at first to help get us off the ground.

Now, you tell me that God's hand was not in all of this. I must reiterate: I am not in charge of this company. Jesus Christ is the Chairman of the Board.

From then on, we started growing and have not stopped. On July 20, 2018, we hit a milestone with $1 billion in assets under management. Now we manage a family of mutual funds and recently launched a few exchange-traded funds (ETFs).

> What have you been called to do? What conviction must you pursue or are pursuing now? No matter how difficult the challenge, we must not give up and we must not compromise, no matter the cost. Remember, obedience trumps performance.

---

[1] Bloomberg Business News, "New Fund Seeks Christians," The News Journal, April 15, 1994.

Bonnie's View:
What's in a Name?

The disciples were called Christians first at Antioch.
—Acts 11:26c

Art often says, if you're going to say you're a Christian or you operate a Christian organization, you had better act like it or change your name. Being Invested with Purpose requires being careful with names. This holds whether we're operating a business, a church, a nonprofit organization or naming our children. What we name a thing or person must be purposeful. If we use a name with any meaning, we must make sure we live up to the name; otherwise, we're hypocritical.

Often, people think Timothy Plan was named after the fund's founder. There was a key person named Timothy, but he was a follower of the Apostle Paul and helped carry out some of Paul's missionary assignments. Why is he Timothy Plan's namesake, and why would the Biblically Responsible Investing Movement's first fund be named after

1994 ART & BONNIE

him? The idea didn't come from Art Ally, but from his wife and partner for more than 58 years—Bonnie Ally.

As Art Ally's wife, Bonnie has been by his side for more than 58 years. She has her own take on what makes him tick and how Timothy Plan came to be. She told their story to Nehemiah Project Founder Patrice Tsague, and here are some excerpts:

A brief Q&A with Bonnie

BONNIE: We've been a part of the church since we've been married. It wasn't until we lived in Boca Raton in late 1987 when we became really involved in the pro-life movement. After we moved back to Orlando in 1990, Art took part in the pro-life rallies here in town. He organized many of the churches and many volunteers for the "Life Chains" where thousands of people lined both sides of Highway 50 holding pro-life signs. It was disappointing that news media only reported a few hundred. However, those who participated knew it wasn't the truth. It seems like Art has always been involved one way or another. Since he accepted Christ, God has been in the center of his life.

PATRICE: I want to know what it was about the pro-life movement that captured your heart in such a strong way? What led you to get involved in the rallies?

BONNIE: Well, although we were active in church, we didn't think too much about abortion. While we were still living in Orlando, we attended a showing of the film "Silent Scream," and it broke our hearts. After moving to Boca Raton, we became aware of a couple of churches that sponsored pregnancy centers and met a few friends who were involved in a pro-life organization. We ended up joining the organization, and it seemed there were rallies every month. We became friends with one of the doctors involved, and now he is one of our partners. It's amazing how God brings you to different people at different times. It touched our hearts, and when we moved back to Orlando, in 1990, Art brought that passion back with him and became even more involved. Our first event was a city-wide rally, and he became chairman of three annual Life Chains and organized thousands of Christians who stood three feet apart along two major Orlando roadways for two hours holding signs, "Abortion kills children" and "Jesus heals and forgives." Because of his involvement in the pro-life movement, a group of pro-life activists suggested Art needed to run for state representative in 1990.

PATRICE: And I know that race kind of became the impetus to launch Timothy Plan.

BONNIE: Right, because he lost the race by six votes. After that, we left it open and available to do other things. Since working with Shearson in Winter Park, they made a new policy that no employee can run for political office again. Art did not like that rule, so he left Shearson and joined Raymond James to start his own independent financial practice, Covenant Financial Management. Through his practice he was helping a lot of pastors. A friend was concerned these pastors did not have anywhere to invest their retirement plan biblically. How can pastors support what they're preaching against? Art searched for retirement plans with clean funds, similar to Timothy Plan, ones screening for unbiblical companies, but there were none. In 1992, his persistent friend asked, "Why don't you start one?" That's how it all began—a seed was planted, or was it a thorn bush? Art said, "I don't really want to start one," he reluctantly took two years to put it together. He was trying to find funds these pastors could invest in that weren't involved in abortion, pornography or alcohol and all those things.

PATRICE: I love it, Bonnie. Because Art has always had a vision, we're going to title this book, "Invested with Purpose," suggesting this commitment Art has had. It seems like even early on, whether it would have been Timothy Plan or something else, he would have found a way to invest in something purposeful.

BONNIE: Correct. Everything he has done confirms it.

PATRICE: Yeah, like Christian movements. Art has a sense of passion and calling to do the Lord's work, would you agree?

BONNIE: Yes, I do. One example was getting involved in a pro-life rally when we lived in Boca Raton. Even Josh McDowell, a Protestant Christian apologist and evangelist, joined us. Events like these fueled Art's passion to continue the fight for the unborn.

PATRICE: Were you conscious of the fact that launching Timothy Plan would mean sacrificing your then-current lifestyle?

BONNIE: We didn't really think about it. Before Timothy Plan, he had a fruitful business, we were living in a nice, big house, and we had a steady, healthy income. It took a real commitment because it would have been easy to just keep going. We had an easy life, making money. I wasn't working; I was content staying at home. We didn't really think about it much. We thought it was going to be well received, thinking it would do well quickly and everything was going to be fine and dandy. Since God called us to do this, things were going to be just fine. But it wasn't easy. Steve took over his financial planning practice, allowing it to remain open, which helped keep us afloat.

PATRICE: How did you come up with the name Timothy Plan?

BONNIE: Art had a friend working for him when he managed the Bache branch in Lexington, Kentucky—Harold Reese—he had written a book called "Financial Bondage." Unfortunately, there was a horrible fatal accident, and Harold died.

Coincidentally, this was close to the time Art was developing the new Christian based mutual fund. When Art asked, "What are we going to call this fund?" We didn't know very much about finances in the Bible. Then I remembered Harold's book. I started looking through it and writing down all the Scriptures having to do with finance. I came up with several verses from the Book of Timothy, so that's how I decided on the name Timothy. Three particular verses felt right: 1 Timothy 5:8: "For if anyone does not provide for his own, and especially those of his household, he has defied the faith and is worse than an unbeliever." That one really hit home and made a case for investing for the future. Also, 1 Timothy 5:22: "Do not lay hands on anyone hastily nor share in anyone's sin. Keep yourself pure." This verse made the case for screening our sin stocks. Finally, 1 Timothy 6:10: "For the love of money is a root of all kinds of evil. For which some have strayed away from the faith and towards greediness and pierced themselves through with many sorrows." That's how I chose the name Timothy, which ended up to become Timothy Plan, by spending time going through this book. It was a good memory of Harold too. I did come up with the name while Art was busy putting all the legal stuff together.

PATRICE: As you said, there was a sense of calling that really came upon you. As you were reading God's Word, is this what drove you to seek the will and truth of God and live it out in your daily lives?

BONNIE: When the opportunity is there and God says "do it," you do it. We were listening for what God wanted us to do, not necessarily going out and trying to save the world. But when people ask you to do things, and you feel the call, you just do it. Art's a great organizer—when he's committed, he can get stuff done very efficiently. When he loves to do something, it gets done.

PATRICE: Bonnie, what were the most exciting periods for you on this journey?

BONNIE: When we first started Timothy Plan, I was working in a church office. When Art began Timothy Partners, Ltd., he needed me, so I left my job at the church and joined the team. It was fun—I was excited to work with Art, Cheryl, and later Steve. We were a small family business initially. Timothy Plan started with just one no-load fund—the Small Cap Value Fund. We were a curiosity, so Art would be interviewed on the radio a lot. We'd get hundreds of calls coming into the office; it was a hectic and exciting time.

We did everything. We answered the phones, we did the mailing, and so much more and at the time it was exhausting. Dave Hart eventually joined the team. With just six at the office, we wore many hats. Those were fond memories for me. Now we have more people to handle the workload.

PATRICE: Did you always believe this was going to work?

BONNIE: I think we always believed it was going to work. You just believe it. Even though you may be tempted to doubt it at times, you just go forward.

PATRICE: How do you feel about where the company is now?

BONNIE: The company is doing great now. Things are at the point where we can sit back and relax. Art can do more macro work now. He's out there doing more promotion. It seems to take forever for people to get to know and trust who you are. We were basically a word-of-mouth business. We didn't have a lot of money to spend on advertising. Basically, God opens the doors and gives us opportunities. Now, I am his partner and here to support him. Art and I travel the world sharing our story with others. In the office, I provide administrative support by paying the bills and serving as office manager. I don't have a securities license. I try to encourage them and be there for them—that is all I do.

PATRICE: That's a whole lot.

BONNIE: We try to never discourage them. Whatever we do, we do as a whole family. We have our entire team, including our kids working here.

PATRICE: What do you think the key to success has been, Bonnie?

BONNIE: Knowing Who's in charge. Every day, we know it's not our business. We are here to serve, and we've made a commitment that God provides, and we give. I don't know how much money Art has budgeted to support various ministries. Since I write the checks, I believe we give away well over 20% of our profits. We rarely increase our salaries. We don't give it to ourselves—we give it to support numerous ministries. It's fun because our entire team knows they have a part in being generous.

PATRICE: And you know my ministry, Nehemiah, has been a beneficiary of your generosity. On behalf of us and many other organizations out there, thank you.

BONNIE: Unfortunately, we have a limited budget, and we do not have millions of dollars to give, hopefully someday we will. Some of the ministries we support include Orange County Jail Ministry, Florida Family Policy Council, Liberty Counsel, numerous pro-life, pro-family ministries, and many others. These essential ministries can't survive without funding.

PATRICE: Is that a sense of responsibility now for you?

BONNIE: It's a responsibility that brings us joy. Art loves giving.

PATRICE: How do you feel about your children being involved?

BONNIE: We feel blessed and they all do something entirely different. Cheryl's been with us since 1992. Steve started to work with Art in Raymond James, probably around 1991. Our oldest son, Doug, had a military career. After serving 21 years in the Navy, he began doing screening research with ICSRI. All three of our children are here, which is exciting. How many people can say that? Although they have conflicts at times, they get along well because they all believe in the mission.

What's in your name? If you're a Christian, are you doing your best to live up to that name? If you were in the Book of Acts with the early Apostles, would they call you a fellow Christian? If you're a Christian operating a business, nonprofit, or church, are you living and operating your business in a manner reflecting the convictions of your faith? If you're a Christian professional or politician, are you carrying out your vocation in a manner reflecting your values? If not, you're not Invested with Purpose.

11

Art's Testimony

I have been crucified with Christ and I no longer live,
but Christ lives in me.—Galatians 2:20a

> Being Invested with Purpose requires a transformed life,
> one under the Lordship of Jesus Christ and His biblical
> teachings. Wherever we are in our spiritual journey,
> we can choose today to submit ourselves to Christ and
> deepen our devotion to His teaching.

I was born in a non-religious home. We weren't Christian, we weren't Muslim, we weren't anything. Fortunately, we had good values and a good home environment.

Nonetheless, I always felt drawn to go to church and knew something was missing in my life. Growing up, I never entered a church except for marriages and funerals until I starting dating Bonnie. We went to her Congregational Church, which was very liberal. We didn't know the difference. Thankfully, we started growing in the Lord anyway.

When we moved to Sherman, Texas, our neighbors invited us to go to a Disciples of Christ church. It was also very liberal. We raised our kids there for years. Even in Lexington, Kentucky, we attended a Disciples church. God works all things together for good.

One member of our Kentucky Disciples church got really excited about a 30-day adventure, so we signed up for it. The program was written by a Sunday school teacher for young adults, Sam Teague, who, one Sunday morning while trying to prepare his lesson had put his head on his kitchen table praying for guidance. In 20 minutes, he wrote a program called "The John Wesley Great Experiment" and over the past 40 years has impacted the world.

It's really pretty simple. You make a commitment for 30 days to do five things. It's not so hard. Anyone can commit to anything for 30 days.

First, dedicate 5:30 a.m. to 6 a.m. every single morning in a structured period of prayerful contemplation. For the first 10 minutes, you write in a diary about how the daily Scripture verse provided applies to your life today. In the second 10 minutes, you write one unpremeditated act of kindness or generosity you will perform for someone that day. The last 10 are the easiest part: You write one thing you want to improve upon in your spiritual life.

This initial step is designed to address our core problem: Who do we think of 95 percent of the time? Ourselves. This puts God first, others second, and yourself last.

Second, commit to tithe—whether you have the money or not—during those 30-days, you simply trust God to provide.

Third, commit to meet as a group weekly to share what's going on as a result of this program. A lot of tears are shed during that meeting. People open up and share what they're finding out during the 30-minute initial period when God puts into their minds someone who needs them—whom they never would have thought about otherwise. When they reach out to a person or simply perform an act of kindness for them, the result really blows them away.

Fourth, volunteer two hours each week to your church.

Fifth, tell at least two people who are not in the program about your experience.

It changed my life. It changed Bonnie's. I claimed Christ as my Lord and Savior before, yet this experiment was really life-changing.

As far as the size of the group, it's recommended to begin with at least 10 but no more than 20. Those whom God draws together have life-changing experiences. In one instance, two people signed up who hated each other. By the conclusion of the 30 days they had become friends. I've seen it happen over and over again—this course really is life-changing.

Yearning for More

Even so, we were still in a Disciples of Christ Church. We were not getting fed, and our hunger to be nourished was growing. When we moved back to Orlando, we re-joined our old Disciples church. We raised our kids in this denomination. We didn't know anything else. I became an elder. My partner told me he heard his pastor preach an outstanding message about the cycles churches go through to alternate between growing and fading. His pastor was J.C. Mitchell of the First Baptist Church of Winter Park.

I called Dr. Mitchell and introduced myself. I told him I was the chairman of the elders at a Disciples of Christ Church in Winter Park and, "frankly, we need your help. I heard about your teaching and wanted to know if you would consider teaching our elders how to become elders." He asked, "What's your pastor say about that?" I said, "Our pastor will attend the meeting. Please come and help us."

Pastor Mitchell came to our elders meeting and did the most masterful job I have ever seen explaining the biblical duties of an elder. I watched to see if it was registering with the others. I watched our pastor, but he was clueless. He didn't know. He didn't care. Next Sunday, at the pulpit he said, "I don't care what the Bible says. There is no devil."

Bonnie and I filled that church with our absence, went to J.C. Mitchell's church and began growing. We grew more spiritually in one month than in all my years in liberal churches.

I became manager of the brokerage office in Boca Raton, and we began looking for a church home. We went to First Baptist Church of Boca Raton because we were now Baptists. We went to the pastor to ask about joining, and he told us, "We have 600 in our church and don't want any more." Stunned by the comment, we ended up joining Spanish River Presbyterian Church (PCA).

After we returned to Orlando, I called J.C., and he said, "Thank goodness. I need you here." Some egomaniacs were giving him fits. We continued on for a couple of years until J.C. stepped down. After a few months, we felt led to seek out another church that better filled our spiritual needs.

We ended up moving our membership to Aloma Baptist Church in Winter Park, where Joe Boatwright was the pastor, and became quite active. Joe wanted to retire, and some wanted elders to help the deacons run the church. They kind of forced Joe out of the 900-member church and appointed 18 people to a search committee. I was elected as chairman but had no idea what I was doing. We spent nearly three months defining what we wanted in a pastor—age range, doctrine, degree, married, children. We started receiving resumes from all over the country. Orlando is pretty attractive to pastors, so we received hundreds of resumes.

And a "Young Child" Shall Lead Them

Meanwhile, I was invited to go to Charlotte, North Carolina, to talk with some conservative Baptist Churches of Virginia who split from the liberal ones. There were 130 churches represented. They wanted me there because they were worried about getting kicked out of the Southern Baptist Convention retirement plan, and Timothy Plan was an alternative.

We met in a Southern Baptist church in Richmond. I recall when a "young child," 28-year-old Anthony George, stood up to preach. He mesmerized the pastors in attendance. I sought him out following his message, introduced myself, and told him I believed God just told me that he was going to be our next pastor at Aloma Baptist Church. He was very comfortable in his current church and had no interest in moving to Orlando.

Although he didn't fit our criteria, the boy could sure preach. I took some of his sermon tapes back to our search committee, but they were evenly split about selecting him. I sent the naysayers up to his church in Virginia to hear him. They came back raving fans.

God kept putting people in Anthony's path who pointed him here. Finally, he agreed to consider it, if it's unanimous. He came down, gave a sermon, and at the business meeting the following week the vote was unanimous in issuing the call.

Anthony spent 15 years at Aloma and doubled church attendance before being called to be Charles Stanley's successor at his church in Atlanta.

This goes to show if you get out of God's way, He will take care of things.

"A Pass-through to Ministries"

Following our experience with The John Wesley Great Experiment, Bonnie and I started doing a Bible study devotion every morning at home and have been doing it for 15 to 20 years or more. We've been doing a Torah study for the last eight years—5:30 to 6 a.m. It's our treasured half hour. We don't miss it.

When things get tough here at Timothy Partners, we understand God can shut it down anytime He wants to. We have had tough times. Our original partners received no return on their investment for 10 years. We have now grown to the point where, last year, we gave over $250,000 to numerous ministries. We see ourselves as a pass-through to ministries impacting the culture.

One of them is Movieguide, Ted Baehr's Hollywood ministry. We eased into sponsorship of Movieguide's annual film awards because we have synergy; they're having an impact on movies, and we're having an impact on finances. The morning after the awards ceremony, Ted always invites supporters to a breakfast and challenges them to make a "faith promise" with the understanding that if God provides, honor the promise. However, if He doesn't, the promise is forgiven. During breakfast, I asked his son, Robbie, "How much did the ministry receive in direct gifts last year over and above the faith promise?"

He said, "About $5,000." I walked up to the microphone and said to the attendees Timothy Plan's distributor will match dollar for dollar whatever you give right now over and above your faith promise. Big mistake. I later asked Ted, and he wouldn't tell me how much was given, so I pressed Robbie, and he said, "They gave $59,000."—which we then had to match.

The point is, Timothy Plan's distributor is an open-handed ministry as well as a business. We are here to support God's kingdom.

The Bible is clear—giving blesses the giver as well as the recipient. When we understand God owns everything, He made the ultimate sacrifice for us, and He wants us to give for His name's sake, we give more joyfully and generously.

A brief Q&A with Art

QUESTION: Where do you think the culture is going?

ANSWER: It's a much deeper question than you posed. Our culture has lost its biblical foundation, and I believe the fault lies at the doorstep of the church. We have been co-opted by the world. As a result, we have no anchor, no plumb line. Francis Schaeffer tried to warn us: "We use terms like 'God' or 'Jesus,' that have no content. We no longer mean the God and Jesus of the Bible but a God and Jesus that we have redefined into our own image."

It seems too many churches have thrown away the Old Testament. Yet, His guidelines for life are still the guidelines for life. The church is not engaging the culture. To solve this problem, I collaborated with Pastor Paul Blair* to start a Florida-based pastor training program. Pastors learn how to Biblically engage the culture and impact their communities. This 2-day biblical training challenges pastors on how to address key cultural, political and societal issues affecting our nation.

I exhorted Pastor Paul Blair to move to Orlando to pastor a new church plant, Liberty Church Orlando. He is dedicated to the Word and hopes to have a significant impact on our local churches. It is encouraging to understand that God does not need to use a majority to fulfill His will. He only needs a few faithful people.

As far as the culture, do I ever see this turning around? No. Could God turn it around? Sure. This nation is soaked with the blood of over 60 million aborted babies, how do you overcome that? We don't follow any of the biblical guidelines at all.

I believe we are in the Last Days, but it doesn't matter to me. I am either going to Him, or He is coming to me. I am going to live in Heaven forever. Do you know how long eternity is compared to how long life on earth is? Our time here is only a blip.

QUESTION: What is the biggest challenge facing our culture today?

ANSWER: Socialism/Communism. It's a godless form of government, and Satan is using it to take over America and the world.

QUESTION: Do you see any bright spots?

ANSWER: Yes. God has his people everywhere. We must continue to keep an eternal perspective. It does not mean we should not engage. We engage here. It doesn't tell us we are going to win, but we will win after all is said and done.

Timothy Plan has now taken a sliver of money out of industries funding evil. It may be just a sliver, but it is a sliver nonetheless.

I get up every morning with total hope because I know Who's in control. I prefer He doesn't treat me like Job, but if He chooses to, that's okay.

My son Steve, who is battling cancer, knows where he is going. Although we're fervently praying for a complete recovery, if God takes him home, he would leave a hole but only for a short time. Not for eternity.

There's nothing special about me. I know Who I trust. My job is to serve Him as best I can.

QUESTION: How do you see the role of Biblically Responsible Investing ("BRI")?

ANSWER: BRI is a tool to put your faith into action. I think it will explode once people go through our Biblical Stewardship study. What I want people to see is that God is still in the miracle business. He has performed miracle after miracle here. I don't think He will shut us down, but if He does, that's okay too.

QUESTION: Did you ever rethink or reverse a Timothy Plan initiative?

ANSWER: Yes. As we were starting to grow to where investors could asset-allocate, I came to understand advisors were selling class B shares. In a nutshell, class B is when an advisor sells it, the client pays nothing, but the fund advances 4 percent to the selling broker. It's very lucrative for the financial advisor who passes on the invisible cost to the investor. The client doesn't know, because he doesn't pay anything up front.

We had a $1 million credit line to offer B shares from one bank after being turned down by 10 other banks. We had a company with no credit, and which ran in the red. The bank that approved us specialized in real estate loans. Although they had rejected several rock-solid real estate deals before considering ours, the committee approved us, which shocked our loan officer.

Unfortunately, some brokers abused the B shares. I think we were the first fund to shut the class down. It appeared it was becoming immoral, so we stopped offering the B shares. Boy, I heard those brokers squawk. It was the right thing to do.

*Paul Blair, a retired offensive lineman with the NFL's Chicago Bears and Minnesota Vikings, pastored Fairview Baptist Church in Edmond, Oklahoma, before coming to the Orlando area to pastor Liberty Church of Central Florida. His testimony can be found at libertychurchorlando.org/paul-blair.

Do you have a personal relationship with the Lord Jesus Christ? Have you allowed that relationship to transform your life and change the way you act and behave? If not, you can start that journey right now by making a commitment to Jesus Christ as your Lord and Savior. Find a Bible-believing and Bible-teaching church where you can grow in the faith. Make Bible reading a daily part of your life so you can grow in the knowledge of Scripture.

"Jammed Through These Keyholes"

Consider it pure joy, my brothers and sisters, whenever you face trials of many kinds—James 1:2

> No great achievement is ever realized without trials. In the journey to being Invested with Purpose, we will face many of them, from economic turbulence to life's disappointments. But we need not fear; God is faithful and will see us through if He finds us faithful. Things may not always work out exactly the way we want them, but they will work out the way God intended them.

As stated earlier, during its first years, Timothy Plan's distributor was often on the edge of survival, and actually ran out of money four times. In each case, sometimes agonizingly close to a financial deadline, a partner, partners, or someone new came through with enough funding to keep the doors open.

Art had no doubt God was behind every reprieve, and each new lease on life for Timothy Plan was a sign to keep going.

"God owns everything, we own nothing. He can't trust us, so He puts us through testing," Art said. "There isn't anything that could happen to destroy my faith in my Lord and Savior. Nothing—because I've been tested."

"I was never scared," Bonnie recalls. "There were a couple of times where we kept running out of money. You can get worried, or trust God to provide. We've always stayed faithful. Skeptics would say 'you can't do it,' but Art would not change what he was doing.

"The serious thing is feeling you might lose someone else's money," she said. "It was scary because people trusted us with a couple of million dollars, which is a lot of money. The SEC will shut you down if you don't have enough money when you're running a Broker/Dealer operation. There are so many regulations, and they have the power to shut a firm down overnight. It was always humbling when the money ran out, and Art had to ask our partners for more. Thankfully, no one lost any money, and they always came through, even in the tough times."

Nonetheless, Art told each of his small staff to keep their resumes handy, in the top left drawer of their desks. It was an order, not a suggestion.

"This had to do with people needing to support their families," Art said. "Of course, it was a small staff during this time. We all needed to make a living. If our firm was shut down, we all had to find a job.

"Trusting the Lord is a little different from presuming upon the Lord. I didn't know if He wanted us to succeed or not or was just giving us another life lesson. The first time we ran out of money was traumatic. I mean, the initial accumulation of partners' money came to a million dollars, and it was gone. They trusted me, but it was gone. How would you feel in that position? It was traumatic.

"The Lord gave me an idea for how to raise some more capital to keep things going. We created a private placement bond which we offered to our existing partners as well as selected Broker/Dealers to offer to their clients.

"We didn't know if it would work or not, but it did work. However, it turned out to be inadequate, and we ran out of money again. It's a very high-cost business. It takes a lot of money to operate a mutual fund. We ran out of money again. That's where God sent some people whom I had no way of even knowing. They came in and said, 'What are you doing and how can we invest in this enterprise?' And that gave us more money.

"By then my confidence was increasing almost exponentially that the Lord was in this. See, we tend to give lip service. The real question we have to ask ourselves is: Do I trust the Lord? 99.9% of the time that's all it is—lip service.

"You gotta be jammed through these keyholes, and it is really a two-fold experience. You learn you can trust Him no matter what. The other side is, He has to know He can trust you. This is why you have to go through these things. At least, that has been my experience."

First Keyhole

"We really hustled and worked hard to gain more assets, because the more assets we had, the less the red ink there was," Art said. "The first time we nearly went broke was kind of interesting. I called Pastor Joe Boatwright and said, "Man we need to get some of these Southern Baptist pastors on board with Timothy Plan. They preach this stuff in the pulpit, but they're not as careful where their retirement dollars and their 403-B retirement plans are invested.'

"I asked him if he could set up an appointment with a leader in the Southern Baptist Convention. He did. Bonnie and I jumped on a plane and went up to meet with him. It was a high anxiety time because it was the first time we had run out of money, and we weren't sure how we were going to keep things going.

"We thought if we could get some high-level support—not for additional partnership capital but some interest in investing biblically—it would be a little easier to increase our mutual fund assets. I met with one of the top leaders in his home church. He knew we were in dire circumstances.

"It was kind of a mixed blessing, meeting with this top guy was a blessing in itself, but not being sure we were going to survive was the other side of the formula. It turned out we became good friends. He was an icon in the Southern Baptist Convention. He had a financial advisor who had no interest in investing in Timothy Plan. Unfortunately, it didn't accomplish my original hope, of transferring some money in, because then other pastors would have followed suit. Fortunately, we wound up raising more funds to keep going anyway."

Second Keyhole

Timothy Plan's distributor again faced bankruptcy, and Art scrambled to sell a second tier of private placements in the limited partnership. People could buy in for as little as $5,000. We were confident as assets grew under management, the partners would get returns on their investment.

As Steve recalls, some of the partners were surprised at the firm's initial tough sledding.

"They're like 'goodness gracious, we may have just thrown our money down a rat hole,'" he said.

"The first time, God gave me a method to raise additional money from existing partners at various levels," Art said. "Some of them were willing, some of them weren't. After the second time, we ran out it was a done deal. The second time, I'm talking to an advisor and he has a pretty wealthy client who had a very strong interest in what we were doing and that client actually came down to my office and we talked about whether he would like to be a partner in this enterprise. He injected some serious money and kept Timothy Plan's distributor going."

Third Keyhole

This began, of all places, on a cruise.

"I was listed as an alternative speaker with a cruise line because they have programs they put on constantly when you're out at sea," Art said. "Sometimes the scheduled speakers cancel or get sick, and they called me to see if I was willing, on such short notice, to be a speaker on their ship. I never had time; I was too busy trying to get this enterprise going.

"I kept turning them down, and finally I got a call on a pretty nice cruise. I figured if I declined again, I would be off the list. Even though it was a tense time, I accepted. I spoke on investing on this two-week cruise. I received no compensation, just a complimentary cabin. I was the only speaker for 14 days. They didn't have any other programs. Everybody on the ship came to my presentation because there was nowhere else to go when you were at sea.

"Bonnie and I enjoy playing bridge. We met a couple on the ship who kept coming to my class, and we wanted to get more acquainted. They loved to play bridge, and we did too. I was committed to not say anything about the need for money or anything about what we do.

"This couple wouldn't let it go; they wanted to know what we did and were very interested as I was explaining it to them. I was not asking for money. They practically insisted and asked, 'How in the world can we be a part of the ownership group of this enterprise?'

"They already had a pretty nice retirement plan, so they ended up transferring about $400,000 into the partnership, which kept us going. The red ink was shrinking, but it was still there, so we ran out of money a fourth time."

That was the New Year's Eve story (Chapter 1).

> What keyholes has God brought you through in your own journey? What lessons have you learned? Remember, the pivotal lesson to going through these keyholes is God learns He can trust us and we can trust Him. We must learn to trust God, no matter what.

13

Humble Beginnings

Do not despise these small beginnings
—Zechariah 4:10a (NLT)

Many of us on a purposeful journey forget our character is sometimes shaped by a humble beginning. How we start is not always how we will end, but we must be willing to pay the price and do what we can until we have better options. The quality of our journey cannot be determined by monetary success or luxurious packaging but rather by the strength of our convictions and the purity of our purpose.

Like all fledgling, underfunded businesses, Timothy Plan had growing pains and problematic experiences after its founding in 1994.

Making It Work

Its first office consist-
ed of a building in Win-
ter Park that had been
a performing arts the-
ater. By all accounts,
it was a creepy place,
with black walls and
ceilings. It oozed a
strange vibe.

THE FIRST TIMOTHY PLAN HEADQUARTERS

Shortly after applying fresh
paint in one of the offices, Cheryl recalls seeing the words "Go
Away" appear as the paint dried. "Our computers kept crashing.
Maybe it was due to the power lines running fairly close to the
front of our building, but it did not explain some of the strange oc-
currences."

The chairs with wheels on them rolled away from desks, although
Steve scoffs somewhat at the suggestion that this indicated some
sort of demonic activity, even though he described the building as
"possessed."

"The place was old and outdated," he said. "It had a crooked
foundation, so the floors were tilted."

The place was so odd they even called in Art's pastor to pray over
the property.

"Yeah, that was the exorcism," said Cheryl laughing, but only half
joking.

To get the building in shape, the whole family and small staff
pitched in. "We had a paintbrush in one hand and fly swatter in the
other" Steve laughed. "We all did. We didn't hire anybody." Terry

Covert recalls everyone participating in revamping the place. They had to work around the building's limitations.

Sinking Floors

"We didn't have a lot of room, and we had a lot of prospectuses," Terry said. "We stored some upstairs. One day, we saw a crack in the wall. We went in the next day, and the crack was even bigger. It turned out the building was so old and the marketing materials were so heavy they were causing the walls to come apart. We had to take the prospectuses back downstairs."

2006 TERRY POINTS TO CRACK IN WALL

"The old office had termites," Bonnie said. "We came in one day and found our conference table covered in termite wings. The room was sinking from the weight of our prospectus and brochure inventory."

It Smelled Like Death

A couple of times, wild animals of some kind died after crawling underneath the building. "It was pretty bad," Terry said. No one in our office volunteered to crawl under the building, so we had to hire a professional. "It was awful," Steve said. According to Cheryl, "I think it was worse for the ones who had to work downstairs. The building had a crawl space and the floors were made of wood. Whenever an animal died under the building, the smell permeated our working environment. In an attempt to make the smell better, someone decided to use a wintergreen disinfectant. Honestly, I am not sure what was worse, the wintergreen smell (nothing like the candy), the rotting animal smell, or the combination of both. I choose both."

Hurricane Preparedness

"When a hurricane hit in 2004, the attorney who served as fund counsel and I went to lunch," Terry said. "We came back and everybody in the office—there were six or seven of us—were all piling stuff up on desks and stuff. We asked why, and they said 'a hurricane is coming!' They were afraid the floor would be flooded. It actually did not happen, but we were taking no chances."

Redeeming the Computers

At Timothy Plan's first headquarters in Winter Park, Terry Covert and Dave Hart had to rewire the entire place in 1995.

"We ran the wires all over the office," Terry said. "There were eight individual strands to each one, and we had to put them in the right order. It was a mess. Eventually, we made them work—again they stopped working."

Dave had a connection with IT professional Nick Butler. Dave recounted, "As a young boy, Nick used to get parts and build working computers. He was a really sharp, self-taught, young man." Dave called Nick, who came in and set things straight.

As a sub-contractor, he helped put the computers on sound footing several times when there was trouble.

Blowing Out the System

"We had a tenant working upstairs," Dave remembers. "Jonathan was in the commercial real estate business. Art rented him a corner office upstairs because he needed space, and we had a little extra. He bought a new computer and asked Art if he could hook his new computer up to our printer, and Art agreed.

"Jonathan had an IT consultant install his computer. Somehow, by tying into our printer, they managed to reformat the entire hard drive on our network. As a result, all of our internal files were gone. He wiped it out from the inception of the company. We could not call financial advisors because we lost all of our contacts stored in our contact management software. We had no way to communicate with them or anybody else.

"This went on for about three days. Although we showed up for work, we couldn't do anything. Art called an IT friend to see if he could help. Well, after three days of down time, Art was open to more ideas. I told Art, 'I know a guy who might be able to help us.' He said, 'Well, call him!' I did, and Nick came in. In three hours he had us up and running. We can joke about it now."

"I remember Nick very well during that time," Cheryl recalls. "My desk was right next to the server. When he came in to save us from disaster, he simply stepped up to the server and started typing a mile a minute. He was mind-blowing."

When the opportunity finally arose, Cheryl suggested Art should offer him a position. Nick is working there today.

"Everybody Did Everything"

"In 1997, we looked at the expense of paying a firm to serve as our distributor. Alternatively, we chose to bring it in-house," Art said.

"The problem was, you had to be a registered Broker/Dealer to serve as distributor," Art said. "We filed with the National Association of Securities Dealers (NASD) which is now known as the Financial Industry Regulatory Authority, Inc. (FINRA)[i] to become a registered Broker/Dealer.

"During this time you had to file in each state individually as well," Terry said. "Art and I flew to Atlanta to meet with FINRA. We then talked to all 50 states. We were approved in every state except Arizona. We gave Arizona what they asked for over and over, to no avail. We finally mailed them a box full of 10 inches of paper. I sent them everything we could find—they finally said yes."

"I ran the Blue Sky requirements from 1997 to 2004," Terry said. "Blue Sky Laws require registering with each state to transact business. I did it all. At the time, I had no idea what to do. You just kind of feel your way through it. It was a significant relief for me, personally, when we transitioned all of it to a service provider to manage.

"We also did the monitoring of all the trades ourselves. We didn't have very many people. We all pitched in and did what was necessary. Although, Art still made the final decisions. Everybody did everything."

Terry recalled enduring intense heat in an upper floor while standing on a ladder, installing lights. "We were even janitors. In fact, two of my three kids did some of the janitorial work for a while," he said.

Presiding over all this was Art, who is an excellent motivator, mover and shaker.

"Art is a conductor," Steve said. "He knows how to put things together, and they end up coming together."

"I think most would agree," added Cheryl with a smile, "whenever physical sweat is involved, Art is the first person offering to provide and pick up food—probably because it gives him an excuse to avoid the sweat!"

As for the building, whatever the staff did to keep it up, it apparently worked, because Timothy Plan's distributor operated there for 13 years before moving their headquarters to Maitland in 2007.

The old building was razed and turned into a McDonald's. The ghosts have since flown away.

Getting on the Map

At first, Timothy Plan didn't really have any like-minded competitors, just plenty of secular competition from established firms. "There wasn't really the concept of BRI in existence back then," Terry said. "It was only us being biblically responsible."

To get on the map, "We made call after call after call," Terry said. "We struggled day by day. When we had a million dollars in assets under management, we thought we were big stuff. We couldn't understand why the big firms wouldn't do business with us," he said, laughing. "Then we got to $2 million, and it was a big deal."

Did you have humble beginnings? Are you still in an early stage of your journey? Excellence is not always rewarded with luxury or material success, especially at first.

If we're Invested with Purpose and trust God, He will provide ways to enable us to improve our conditions. We shouldn't spend above our means to prove anything nor get into unnecessary financial debt.

[i]   FINRA: a private corporation that acts as a self-regulatory organization. FINRA is the successor to the National Association of Securities Dealers, Inc. and the member regulation, enforcement and arbitration operations of the New York Stock Exchange. From the FINRA website: "In 2017, through our aggressive vigilance, we brought 1,369 disciplinary actions against registered brokers and firms. We levied $64.9 million in fines. And we ordered $66.8 million in restitution to harmed investors. We also referred more than 850 fraud and insider trading cases to the SEC and other agencies for litigation and/or prosecution."

14

Finishing the Race

I have fought the good fight, I have finished the race,
I have kept the faith—II Timothy 4:7

> In our pursuit of being Invested with Purpose, we must be committed to the end no matter how difficult the journey. Our commitment and enthusiasm will inspire others to come alongside us to help us finish the race. That was the case with Timothy Plan and the Biblically Responsible Investing Movement.

The world-famous Indianapolis 500 auto race is held every year on Memorial Day at Indianapolis Motor Speedway, known widely as "the Brickyard."

For a few years, Orlando had its own Indy-style racetrack dubbed the "Mickyard" because of its proximity to Walt Disney

1995: ART ALLY NEXT TO JONATHAN BYRD'S INDY RACECAR

World. It attracted the best drivers in the world and is remembered, probably not so fondly, by the firm's partners because of their unusual experience. Built in 1995 by a subsidiary of the Indianapolis Motor Speedway Corporation, the Mickyard's name was actually Walt Disney World Speedway. The Indy Racing League Indy Car Series kicked off the track's heyday on January 27, 1996, with a 200-mile race, won by driver Buzz Caulkins of Bradley Motorsports with a Reynard chassis and a Ford engine.

Partner Jonathan Byrd, owner of Jonathan Byrd's Racing, had a car in the 1996 race driven by famed Indy race winner Arie Luyendyk, a native of the Netherlands. Known as "the Flying Dutchman," Arie won the Indianapolis 500 in 1990 and in 1997 and was inducted into the Motorsports Hall of Fame in 2014.

In 1997, Byrd's Racing had a car in another 200-mile Indy-style race at the Mickyard. The partners were invited to attend the event in conjunction with their annual meeting.

Jonathan Byrd was a devout Christian who had become a legend in the restaurant business in Indiana. After growing up working in his family's custard stand, Jonathan branched out and became known for serving fried chicken. After a personal visit from Col. Harland Sanders, Jonathan and his wife Ginny became major franchisees of Kentucky Fried Chicken, and they eventually opened a cafeteria and other food businesses.

"Whenever he was given the opportunity, Jonathan Byrd would always talk about all of the significant events of the Bible, and of the life of Christ, involving food," according to his obituary in the Indianapolis Star, penned by his son David.

"There were the occasions of the feeding of several thousand people, the story of the resurrected Savior cooking fish for his disciples on the shore of the Sea of Galilee, and of course, the meal of the Last Supper, when Jesus shared the mystery and the power of Him sacrificing His body and His blood for the salvation of the world. There was power in those events, and Jonathan realized very early on in life, there is something significant, and something very special, about serving people food."

Jonathan was especially supportive of Art's vision for Timothy Plan. "He helped Art get it started," David Byrd said. "My Dad and my grandmother invested in the limited partnership with a 10% share."[1]

Jonathan was also a trusted advisor. "Early on, Art Ally had great enthusiasm," David said. "He thought wealthy Christians, denominations, churches, and foundations that were faith-based would all flock to Timothy Plan and that it would grow like wildfire.

"My Dad helped temper his enthusiasm, telling him it would be slower growth, month by month, year by year, but that over time, it would do well. Of course, ultimately it would be blessed, and now it's the largest of its kind. Christians can rest easy in good conscience, knowing they are invested biblically."

Jonathan Byrd did something else to give Timothy Plan a promotional boost.

"Out of his love, Mr. Byrd put Timothy Plan's logo on the fin of his Indy car. It was a very generous gesture," Steve Ally recalled.

A Wonderful Time—at First

Going to the Indy-style event at the Mickyard in 1997 "was a huge deal for us, since we had a horse in the race, so to speak," Steve said.

On race day, the partners had to park a long distance away, because of congestion generated by the track being too close to the theme parks.

Still, everyone was excited to be there. It was great fun at first. The partners were allowed into the pit. They ate with the drivers and sat in the stands near the track.

"It was noisy," Terry Covert recalled. "We were low in the stands, not knowing the best seats were the higher ones."

Also, "Indy cars have open wheels, so rubber tire debris came flying off the track at us," Steve said.

As the race went on, the temperature dropped, the wind picked up, and clouds gathered. Raindrops began falling. When the cars had completed about three-quarters of the 200 miles, the heavens dumped a torrential downpour. Soggy spectators bolted and ran to their vehicles—a mile away.

Eddie Cheever of Team Cheever, in a G-Force chassis and an Aurora engine, completed 149 miles and was declared the winner. Jonathan Byrd's Racing's driver, Mike Groff, finished second.

The race fans would never forget their decidedly un-sunny Florida experience. "By the time it took 20 minutes to get to our cars," Steve said, "we were soaked and freezing cold." He added with a laugh, "So from then on, getting the partners to come to a future race was not as easy as the first one."

Terry and his wife Sandy fared much better than the rest of the contingents. "We left a little early because my wife is not much of a racing enthusiast," Terry said. "We had parked a little closer and got to the car just as the deluge hit."

As for the Mickyard, it was the site of three more annual 200-mile Indy car races and was also used for the Richard Petty Driving Experience, a program allowing the public to drive NASCAR cars around the track or ride with a professional driver.

Steve drove over to the track one day to see the action. "They were testing, and I was right at the edge of the track where they were going around at more than 100 mph. It was an adrenalin rush, even though it was not the smartest thing to do."

The track permanently closed in 2015 and was razed to make room for more Disney World parking.

Jonathan Byrd passed away at age 57 in August 2009, but his sons David and Jonathan Byrd II along with Jonathan's wife Ginny manage the racing team, which competes in the Indianapolis 500 and other races and still has Timothy Plan's logo on all its cars. Sometimes it's on a fender, sometimes on another part of the car.

"It moves around, depending on what I think is best," David said. "We have Indy cars, sprint cars, midget cars, Silver Crown cars—it's on all of them. In fact, it's on more cars than ever before. The more people who know about Timothy Plan, the more they'll invest, and the more it will grow."

Art is still in awe of the Byrd family patriarch's Christian service.

"Jonathan Byrd likely supported more ministries and gave away more Bibles than any other man on earth," Art said. "He was a man who achieved a very high level of success in business, yet it was his passion for God that marked his life, particularly through generosity.

"We are all blessed to have known such a servant of God. He not only caught the vision of Timothy Plan, but also put his money where his convictions were and became a significant investor in our fund at its launch."

Are you committed to finishing the race? We all must consider what to do in the days and months ahead to make sure we can say we finished our race when the Lord calls us home. It's not how we started but how we end that matters most. Jonathan Byrd finished his race. Art Ally is still running his race. We must be committed to finishing our own race well.

---

[1] David Byrd, in a telephone interview with Robert Knight on March 12, 2019.

15

A Pocketful of Miracles

"I am the LORD, the God of all mankind. Is anything too hard for me?—Jeremiah 32:27

If we don't believe in miracles, we'll have a hard time being Invested with Purpose. There are times when human efforts fail, and good things happen that are inexplicable, illogical, or incomprehensible. Miracles are when God moves on our behalf after we've hit our limit. Many miracles were experienced in its first 25 years. This chapter summarizes some key miracles without which the company would not have survived.

Art remembers five miracles that kept Timothy Plan's distributor going despite daunting odds:

Miracle No. 1: God Brings a Money Manager

During our formative stage, we had a commitment from an existing money manager to serve as our sub-advisor. Throughout the initial period, I called them several times to confirm their commitment to serve in this capacity. I called the manager right before we were ready to launch, and he informed me his committee had decided it would be best if they didn't get involved with us, as it could create problems with some of their other clients due to our abortion screen. There I was, ready to go to press, and I didn't have a money manager. Within 30 minutes of the conversation with the manager who withdrew, a representative of another money manager—who had no idea what we were up to—walked into my office.

I knew him as a representative of the firm that just turned us down. That's when he told me he had stopped in to let me know he had moved to another money management firm and thought I might be interested. If he had walked in 45 minutes earlier, we would have thanked him for coming by and sent him on his way. God sent him in the nick of time.

I was really impressed by his new firm, jumped on a plane, and flew to New Jersey to meet with them. As a result, we agreed they would be our money manager.

Originally, we launched Timothy Plan as a no-load fund, not only for pastors, but for all Bible-believing Christians. This was because we didn't think money-motivated financial advisors would be interested in offering our fund to their clients.

We realized, as a no-load fund, we would have to market it ourselves. We started aggressively calling churches and pastors to let them know it was available. Unfortunately, it didn't seem to register with them. We grew very slowly and knew we had to do something to increase distribution. Within a year, we converted to a load fund so financial advisors who sold our shares could be paid. Even then, we were still bleeding red ink. Asset growth did not happen as quickly as we had expected. The Lord and I talked a lot during those years.

Miracle No. 2: God Writes a Study Guide

That's when it hit me: *They don't know!*

All our training about handling money comes from the world, not the Bible. I had to write a biblical stewardship study.

It took three months, and I wrote it in my bedroom office at home. First, I called Randy Alcorn and asked him to be co-author, but he was too busy. I said, "Well, then, I'm going to steal some of your material to include in this course." He said, "Go for it."

I used his book "Money, Possessions and Eternity" among numerous other sources—the Bible was the core. I wanted to make it easy reading, fun and practical. I didn't write it—the Holy Spirit did. I am not a writer. Upon the conclusion of writing the course, we invited a group of financial advisors to participate in a beta test to get their feedback. They sat through nine hours of this new material in a day and a half, and their critiques proved invaluable.

We received one suggestion from Glenn Repple—who has his own Christian Broker/Dealer—I have held against him ever since. He thought the course would be improved by filming a couple to share their thoughts while going through the course, something that was going to cost a lot more money.

Kim Billips referred her friends, a couple who had started a video production company. They agreed to film our presentation. This low budget production included the parents of the film producer, who were not professional actors.

We gave them the fictional names of Tim and Julie, and they did a great job. I learned in real life, Tim was the regional manager for Krispy Kreme Donuts. It is always good to know a guy like that!

Our purpose for this project was to wake up the body of Christ on how to handle money biblically. I was excited. I've trained over 1,000 advisors to equip them to go to the churches in their communities and educate Christians on biblical stewardship. They all were excited, went home, and knocked on church doors. The church doors did not open. They became discouraged and went back to doing business as usual.

Meanwhile, Timothy Plan's growth continued to struggle. We had a problem. Since asset allocation is the key to successful investing, we had to diversify. Since we had only one fund in which to invest your money biblically, why bother since the rest of your money would have to be invested in unscreened funds? It was clear we had to expand even though we were losing money.

Miracle No. 3: God Gives Art Another Plan

After running out of money the first time, we raised another half million dollars from a private placement bond offering. I wrote a prospectus for this and built in a commission for brokers.

Then, when the money ran out, we went back to our partners and told them we're either going to have to close down or raise more money, so we raised more through a private placement second tier equity offering as well as from a couple of partners and some new people whom God led me to.

Miracle No. 4:
Cruising Into Dollars

I was on a Princess cruise list as an alternative speaker to teach investing. This story can be found in Chapter 12, "Jammed Through These Keyholes."

Miracle No. 5: Attracting Managers with Virtually No Incentives

I knew Timothy Plan had to expand, and we had to change managers in our original Small-Cap Value Fund. After inquiring with several of my Wall Street friends for recommendations, the consensus seemed to suggest Awad and Associates. I went to New York and hired Jim Awad and Associates to replace our original manager.

I knew we had to expand, so I contacted our institutional consultants in Atlanta to help us find appropriate money managers.

I told them up front, "You might find this challenging since I can't afford to pay you any search fees. Also, our biblical screens will probably restrict the companies they normal invest in. We can only afford to pay half of what most managers charge their best clients, and we will begin with no assets in the fund."

They said, "Let us get this straight: You want a manager for a large-medium cap fund and a fixed income fund, and you're going to tie their hands with screening? And start with no money? You're nuts."

They agreed to attempt a search and ended up recommending a manager for each of the two funds. They invited me to Atlanta, where I met with the managers, explained to them our limitations and restrictions, and they both agreed to manage our funds even though we started with no money. The consultants nearly fainted. They had never seen anything like it. I told them Jesus was chairman of the board, and after that, they believed it. They were believers, but now they are Believers with a capital B.

As far as the four times we almost went broke, the first time I was a wreck. The second time they trusted me. The third time I thought, "God wants this," and the fourth time was New Year's Eve, as explained in Chapter 1.

I try not to presume anything, however, I knew the phone would ring. We kept our resumes in our top left-hand drawer because we figured we might have to look for other employment to support our families. The phone rang and it was a partner who had come into money and wanted to invest. That's when I knew God finally had confidence in us.

Six months after Timothy Plan launched, the SEC announced they were going to audit us.

No fund ever gets audited within its first couple of years. The auditor who came appeared to be antagonistic and did not like what we were doing. She was convinced she could shut us down due to inadequate capital (and, she was almost right). We had to report our capital position to her every month, and every month we managed to squeak by.

One Other Trial—The Demonic Woman

A year later, another woman from the SEC came in, and she started throwing her weight around. She was so rude and demanding that Bonnie, who was serving as our office manager, was in tears. She was here for a full week and began to demand records the SEC classified as optional or unnecessary. I gave her only what the SEC required and drew the line at her demand for optional things. At the end of the week, we had our closing conference (just her and me), and it was the worst mistake I ever made—I didn't have any witnesses with me.

In that meeting, she demanded I give her those (non-required) records immediately. She actually hissed at me. That has never happened to me before, and it felt like I was looking into the face of Satan. She said, "We know you Christians. We know what you're up to, and we're going to take you down." It sent chills down my back. I told her, "Get out of my office now!" After she left, I called our fund counsel, advised him I threw an SEC auditor out of my office, and asked if I was in trouble. He nearly fainted.

Three years later, the next team of auditors from the SEC came up, and they were friendly people. It is rare to get audited twice in the first few years.

Whether you believe in miracles or not, they're essential to being Invested with Purpose. We each face a wall or limits along our journey and will need God to intervene. Do you have your own miracle stories of what God has done in your life? What miracles are you expecting? Remember, there's nothing too hard for Him.

16

Selling the BRI Vision

Go, sell the oil and pay your debts.—II Kings 4:7b

Many people don't like the word "sale," however, without sales, great ideas don't see the light of day. It's one thing to have a vision, and it's another thing to sell your idea to people. No matter how powerful your purpose or righteous your vision, if you can't sell it, you won't succeed.

In 1999, Art hired Dave Hart as Timothy Partners' first salesperson. Today, he runs eVALUEator. Previously, he was pivotal in putting Timothy Plan on the map during its crucial growth period.

"I had been in sales my whole life," Dave says. "I sold everything—posters, bread, potato chips, farm equipment, vacuum cleaners, cars—you name it, I sold it. I was selling life and health insurance when I moved back to Florida. I even became involved in some network marketing."

In the early days, we struggled to convince Christian financial advisors they needed to add a biblically responsible element to their product mix.

"Rejection is not a problem for me," Dave says. "I feel whenever anybody rejects what I'm telling them, there are only four possible things could have taken place:

1) I didn't give them enough information;
2) They're not the person I need to be talking to;
3) They don't understand;
4) Or they're not a Christian.

"My slogan for many years has been SWSWSWN: Some will. Some won't. So what? Next.

"Art and I first became acquainted at church where he was my Sunday School teacher. I was selling cars at a local dealership at the time.

"Financially, things were not going well for me. When I joined the firm, Art was not able to fully support me yet. I continued selling cars part-time for almost two years.

"I felt God was in control. Whenever we found ourselves in any tight spot, we could feel the presence of God. Sometimes all you could do is say, 'Wow.'

"Got Some Ministry to It"

"I went through one of the hardest years of my life financially with my business and everything else. It was terrible. I had prayed with my wife and said, 'Debbie, I need to find something with some ministry to it.'

"After trying to sell Art a car, I said, 'Art you're around a lot of people in the Christian community. I'm looking for something that has some ministry to it. Art looked at Bonnie and said, 'Bonnie, this is what we've been praying for.'

"He said, 'Come in and see if you are interested in working with us.' I said okay and ended up joining the firm. For my first assignment, Art wanted me to fill the first National Association of Christian Financial Consultants conference. I called the 250 Christian advisors who had established relationships with Timothy Plan's team. It was people like Steve Ally and Geoffrey Murvin who did the hard work of pre-qualifying the list of Christian advisors. From the list, I was able to convince 99 to attend the first conference. It was a win for our whole team.

"One day, I walked into Art's office and said, 'Art, I really like what we do here, but I need you to understand one thing, I don't do paperwork.'

"Art said, 'Okay.' They started giving me all these forms to fill out. It didn't take him too long to see the wisdom of not giving me any paperwork.

"I knew we needed to raise additional money to keep us in business. My assignment was to sell a private placement in order to raise more equity. I didn't have any idea what a private placement was, but I knew how to sell. We had to increase the capitalization of Timothy Partners by raising another $1 million by selling partnership units for $5,000 apiece.

"I began calling people. It took about 30 days to raise the money. Time went on, and we ran out of money again. We had to offer a second private placement to existing partners. These private placements kept us in business because we were going into the red every month."

Gaining Momentum

In 2003, Timothy Partners finally broke-even. The days of seeking more money were finally behind us. The many and varied challenges of introducing a new product were demanding: teaching the concept to advisors, marketing to the public, and explaining the benefits of investing biblically. Finally, it matured. The road to success was long but worth every step.

Building the Army

"In the beginning, finding Christian financial planners was one of our biggest challenges," recalls Steve Ally. "Finding our target market—Christians interested in investing—was our top priority. In the '90s, uncovering this group of planners took quite a bit of creativity and diligence. We scoured the country for Christian business directories like the Shepherd's Guide, The Blue Book, Christian Businessman Association, The Yellow Pages, and many others. We would search in the Financial Planning, Investment, and Insurance sections and contacted each person one-by-one.

Then we would look further and contact the companies listed to encourage them to tell their financial planner about Timothy Plan and Biblically Responsible Investing.

Later, we used the internet to find Christians in the financial planning field by searching with keywords (e.g., stewardship, Kingdom, Christian, agape, etc.).

National Association of Christian Financial Consultants

We began to build relationships with Christian financial advisors. Art felt the need, with the prodding of financial advisor Mark Minnella, to get them to come together to learn from each other, fellowship with one another, and grow the movement together. The National Association of Christian Financial Consultants (NACFC) was born in 1999.

ATTENDEES AT NACFC'S 3RD ANNUAL CONFERENCE

Illustrating the Story

"In the early days, eVALUEator was the tool we used when talking to financial advisors and even investors about investing in Timothy Plan," said Dave Hart.

eVALUEator is a program for financial advisors to create "moral reports" for their clients. This analysis illustrates how an investment portfolio aligns with their clients' values.

"Through eVALUEator," Dave continued, "we now had an effective way to show people the whole story. I was able to show them precisely what was in their portfolios."

Adding New Funds

Timothy Plan really began to see success with the launch of additional mutual funds and finding managers for these funds with the help of our institutional consultants in Atlanta. Imagine, if you will, attempting to find a fund manager willing to take on a mutual fund that limits what they can buy, and can't promise what they do buy will not eventually fail our biblical screening criteria. With Timothy Plan's variety of funds, we could now offer advisors a way to diversify within the same fund family and get access to Kingdom Class fund management at the same time.

The Lipper Award

"When I started in 2006, we truly hit a home run," said Brian Mumbert, Vice President of Financial Advisor Relations. "We were informed we had won a Lipper Award for our Large/Mid Cap Value Fund for its performance in 2005. Being new to the business, it was great for me to pick up the phone and have advisors express how well they thought our funds were doing. It was such an exciting time to experience success in reaching advisors all over the country who years ago had balked at working with us previously."

Market Collapses

Little did we know what lurked around the corner in 2008. The financial crisis was something that could have put all this to an abrupt halt. Timothy Plan kept setting internal records for all-time highs in assets under management, and then almost overnight close to 40% of our assets under management had been wiped away by the market crash. "I had only known positive performance and advisors eager to hear about Timothy Plan at this point in my career," says Brian Mumbert. "Now advisors were running scared of phone calls, and the ones that did answer were searching for answers.

"We spent time praying with advisors, praying for our shareholders, and praying for our jobs. I remember Art holding a meeting with us, and he asked if we would all consider pay cuts to keep everyone employed. One by one we would go into his office and tell him the very lowest salary we could take and still pay all of our bills. To see that kind of commitment, it was truly humbling. Even with the decline of assets, not one employee was let go."

The faith of Timothy Plan shareholders has been unprecedented. "I have seen the market go up and the market go down, especially on September 11, 2001, as a result of the attack on America and the 2008 Financial Crisis after Congress rejected the bank bailout bill," remembers Debbie Hart, Vice President of Investor Relations. "It has brought joy to my life witnessing the commitment our shareholders have with Timothy Plan. Most believe as the Bible teaches— all the financial resources they have are due to the Lord's provision. Therefore it is not their money but His, and they are called to be faithful stewards of that provision. When the market goes down, investors often recoil from their current mutual fund and jump to another. However, our shareholders remained steadfast because of the commitment they have to our screening process and to their desire to handle God's money His way."

"At times, shareholders would call the office directly to let us know they were praying for Timothy Plan," Brian recalls. "God truly had His hand on all of this."

Adding ETFs to the Mix

"To continue our mission of providing Christians with relevant investment products that do not compromise their biblical values, we partnered with Victory Capital to launch two ETFs," Art Ally confirms. "Victory Capital provides the level of service and expertise Timothy Plan investors expect, and I feel confident Victory Capital can help us fulfill our highest priority—to glorify God by striving for excellence in all that we do." On April 30, 2019, Timothy Plan launched two biblically responsible ETFs to give investors more choices.

ETFs are an affordable, transparent, tax-efficient, and simple way to passively invest and steward God-given resources wisely.

> How well are you doing at selling your vision? Proverbs 29:18 says, "Where there is no vision, the people perish: but he that keepeth the law, happy is he." It's clear how important it is to have a vision from the Lord. Take a minute and meditate on the Word and ask the Lord for wisdom about your life's vision.

17

The Screening Process

*Better a little with righteousness than much gain
with injustice.—Proverb 16:8*

> Being Invested with Purpose requires aligning our
> time, talents, and treasure. Our time must be used in
> doing things to bring about the will of God on earth.
> Our talents must be used to glorify our Lord. Our
> treasure must be used to build His Kingdom and not
> wittingly—or unwittingly—advance the adversary's
> agenda.

Since 1993, the screening process has been an integral part
of Timothy Plan. Before the fund even launched, Cheryl began
compiling research from ministries such as Life Decisions International and American Family Association. Cheryl recalls,

"We were still living in the DOS world, and the internet was not exactly accessible to the average person. At the time, I remember using WordPerfect for DOS to record every finding those ministries listed in their publications. I tracked changes whenever a new publication arrived in the mail. Art used this data to test the possibility of starting a non-denominational Christian mutual fund.

"Over the years, so much has changed and improved. Shortly after moving into our first office building, we upgraded to Windows 95. Wow, I had no idea how wonderful it would be to see things beyond orange and black. It was a whole new world for me and for the screening research. I moved everything to Microsoft Excel, and my need for organization was satisfied.

"Our sources for research also changed with the increased accessibility of the internet. The information we were able to capture made research even more demanding. Since my position required me to balance multiple jobs including answering the phone, building our first website, and creating advertisements, I knew my plate was too full to properly focus on research. We passed the responsibility on to someone who could devote their entire time to research. I often performed random audits to try and catch anything which might have been overlooked."

The research began as a DOS document, moved to Excel for many years, and as it grew with increasing detail and retention of historical violations, the file size became too large for Excel, crashing daily. In an attempt to streamline the process, a new database was designed by Mike Adamission, the developer of what is now eVALUEator.

Timothy Plan screens are now managed at the Institute for Corporate Securities Research, Inc. (ICSRI) by Douglas Ally and his team of researchers. ICSRI is fully integrated into eVALUEator, allowing research results to be reflected in real time. Once the word got out, financial advisors began clamoring for the research to be made publicly available. "The research was our lifeblood, so we held it close to our chests. It set us apart," said Steve Ally.

In 2011, ICSRI made its equities research available to eVALUEator subscribers through the INVESTigate tool. Today, the BRI movement has expanded to include several money management firms nationwide who use this tool to screen holdings.

The Screens

In 1994, Art pioneered the first pro-life, pro-family screening standard. Timothy Plan's commitment is first to the Lord, and will not invest a single penny into any company violating their screens.

The screens were created based on the following core beliefs:

> We believe our bodies and the lives we lead are gifts from our Creator. A healthy biblical lifestyle is a life free from addiction, participation in activities posing potential harm to ourselves or others, and sexual impropriety. Alternatively, a healthy biblical lifestyle protects the sanctity of marriage and sexuality, promotes care of our bodies, assists those who struggle with substance abuse, and strives to promote justice and equality for our most vulnerable.

> We understand the screens we choose to focus on may not appeal to everyone. And some may even find them controversial. All of our screens are based on how Scripture instructs us to live. Our purpose is not to judge the person, but to avoid the actions that cause His people to stumble. Our hope is that no matter your views, one can respect our desire to please the Lord in all we do and say.

LIFE

ABORTION: Life is a precious gift from God—even from the moment of conception. This screen seeks to protect the life of the unborn by screening out companies involved in the abortion industry, including fetal tissue research and the manufacturing and distribution of abortifacients.

ABORTIFACIENT   DISPOSAL
CLONING   PHILANTHROPY
FETAL TISSUE   PROMOTE
HOSPITAL

PURITY

PORNOGRAPHY: Our culture has exchanged true beauty and sexuality for the lust of the eyes and impurity—and seeks to make it a commodity. This screen identifies companies engaged in the promotion of adult themes through advertisements, media, games, stores, establishments, publications, and the internet.

ADVERTISER   PHONE
AUDIO   PRINT
FILM   RETAIL
GAMES   TELEVISION
INTERNET   THEATER

FAMILY

ENTERTAINMENT: Families are the foundation of our culture, and the values we instill need to be preserved. This screen identifies companies engaged in anti-family entertainment through the promotion of violence, language, sex and drugs through advertisements, media, games, stores, establishments, and publications.

ADVERTISER	INTERNET
AUDIO	PHONE
ESTABLISHMENT	PRINT
FILM	RETAIL
GAMES	TELEVISION

MARRIAGE

LIFESTYLE: Marriage is holy—instituted by God. This screen filters to recognize companies that affirm the marriage covenant, a sacred bond between a man and a woman instituted by and publicly entered into before God.

ADVERTISER	PHILANTHROPY
AUGMENTATION	PRINT
ESTABLISHMENT	PROMOTE
LEGISLATION	SPONSOR

LIBERTY

RIGHTS: We are endowed by our Creator with certain inalienable rights—life, liberty, and the pursuit of happiness. These rights are removed from many people across the world. This screen identifies companies that are involved in human oppression, human trafficking, slave labor, terrorism, and Christian persecution.

ARMING TERRORISTS   PERSECUTION

LABOR EXPLOITATION   TERRORIST

STEWARDSHIP

GAMBLING: We are called to be wise stewards with all that God has given us— not as one who gambles away his money or brings himself to ruin. This screen identifies gambling related activities, including equipment manufacturers, casinos, riverboats, cruise lines, racetracks, and gambling software.

EQUIPMENT   PHONE

FACILITY   SERVICES

INTERNET   TELEVISION

LONGEVITY

TOBACCO: It's a silent killer and a common cause of lung cancer, so we do not invest in companies that manufacture tobacco. This screen identifies manufacturers of cigarettes, cigars, smokeless tobacco products, tobacco leaf distributors and marketers, and tobacco specific retail stores.

PRODUCT

DISTRIBUTOR

RETAIL

CANNABIS

SOBRIETY

ALCOHOL: Alcohol addiction hurts and destroys children and families; therefore, we do not invest in companies that manufacture alcohol. This screen identifies companies that enable these abuses, including brewers, distillers, microbrewers, and winemakers.

BREWER

DISTILLER

DISTRIBUTOR

EQUIPMENT

MICROBREWER

RETAIL

WINEMAKER

Screening Accountability

Over the years, the screens have grown and adapted to the culture. Currently, these screens consist of five cultural screens and three social screens having multiple subcategories.

Companies with one or more violations are removed as an investment option. This information is actively updated and communicated to the Timothy Plan fund managers for compliance and accountability.

Each fund is spot-checked to determine whether a company in the portfolio has recently engaged in an activity violating the screens. Timothy Plan has a strict screening policy on any company violating the screens; in other words, if any company currently owned is determined to be in violation, it is liquidated as soon as practically possible, keeping, of course, the interests of our shareholders as our primary concern.

eVALUEator has been an essential tool to ensure Timothy Plan funds stay clean. As of 2019, other investment firms are also using this service to help screen their investments, including Eventide, Aris Corporation, Baptist Life Association, CFD Investments, G.A. Repple, Christian Wealth Management, FlexPlan, OneAscent, and several foundations.

Knowing What You Own

Whether you are new to the faith or are mature in your Christian walk, selecting a mutual fund should be about more than its rate of return—it should also complement your faith.

Until the creation of eVALUEator, it was difficult for individuals to know how to align their investments with their values.

Viewing a screen report of a mutual fund can be an eye-opening experience. Christians work hard to abstain from sin in areas encountered daily. Parents are generally on guard to protect children from the impact of the culture.

It is easy to lose sight of the bigger picture when it comes to investing. Tobacco companies pay high dividends to shareholders, and yet return no redeemable value to society. Once viewed, an eVALUEator report cannot be placed back in a box. It has a way of exposing personal idols, particularly when it comes to money and stewardship.

Brennan Manning stated: "The greatest single cause of atheism in the world today is Christians who acknowledge Jesus with their lips and walk out the door and deny Him by their lifestyle. That is what an unbelieving world simply finds unbelievable." Investing as the secular world does while claiming God owns it all very much denies Christ with our lifestyle.

Do you know what you own?

What is eVALUEator

eVALUEator was the start of a new movement.

"There were some funds screened for alcohol, tobacco, and gambling, but that was it," recalled Dave Hart, who runs eVALUEator.

Art met with a financial advisor who had the vision to create a software program comparing screens based on American values against mutual fund holdings. The reports generated a transparent view of the violation of the underlying holdings of mutual funds.

Timothy Partners collaborated with eVALUEator by providing their research to expand the software to include Timothy Plan's biblical screens.

"The original owner decided to sell eVALUEator to Timothy Partners," Dave continued. "Knowing the potential positive impact it could have on the investment industry, Art asked three of our original partners about buying eVALUEator."

Over the years, there has been heavy investment into upgrading it into the very sophisticated version it is today. eVALUEator uses Morningstar®[1] as its fund data provider. The process of importing mutual funds, ETFs, bond funds, and variable annuities is accomplished using a complex, custom-coded, autonomous importer built into eVALUEator and was redesigned by professional software developer Mike Adamission of Precision Infinity.

In 2019, eVALUEator had almost 10,000 funds containing over 555,000 individual securities. A security can be listed in Morningstar® in multiple ways, depending on how the funds report their holdings, essentially creating duplicate entries. Through an exhaustive process, those securities are individually linked to their respective parent company, sometimes automatically and sometimes manually.

The screening research company, ICSRI, manages over 37,800 companies. During an average update, over 555,000 holdings have to be filtered into 37,800 parent companies. Without this procedure, it would be impossible to accurately show the percentage of violations or the amount of assets each fund might have.

To complicate things further, many investment funds contain other funds within their holdings, which also hold multiple securities, and so on.

Let us look at an example of one complexity both eVALUEator and ICSRI successfully solve daily.

- 21st Century Fox America has over 40 different publicly traded bond offerings, held across numerous funds

- Although a privately owned company, 21st Century Fox America is a subsidiary of publicly traded Walt Disney Co.
- These securities must all be linked to symbol DIS - The Walt Disney Co.

Every 90 days eVALUEator imports information from market data researcher Morningstar® and cross checks the holdings against the ICSRI research. When a new holding is discovered, ICSRI checks to see if any screen violations are found. INVESTigator is a subset of the eVALUEator tool and provides the individual research findings of ICSRI.

Basic information is available to individuals for free at moralinvesting.com.

> How committed are you to being Invested with Purpose? Are your time, talents, and treasures fully aligned with your convictions? Have you evaluated your investments to make sure you're not funding the very things that violate your faith?

---

[1] The portfolio holdings provided in eVALUEator are obtained from Morningstar®, Inc. ("Morningstar®") as of the date reflected in eVALUEator; Morningstar® assumes no liability for the accuracy of the data contained herein, including errors and omissions, the timeliness of the data disseminated, and the opinions expressed. Morningstar® has asserted and maintains all proprietary rights in the Morningstar® Data. The information provided by eVALUEator is not intended as investment advice. It is intended to assist persons to become more informed about their investment portfolios and the investment vehicles being considered for their investment portfolios. Neither eVALUEator nor Morningstar® make any warranties of any kind, either express or implied, including any warranty of merchantability or fitness of Morningstar® Data and other information for any particular use or uses.

eVALUEator

eVALUEator compiles research of almost 10,000 investment products.

The Basics:

- Utilizes Morningstar Fund Data
- Complements Morningstar Reports
- Realigns Clients' Portfolios with their Values

eVALUEates:

- Open-Ended Mutual Funds
- Fund of Funds
- Bond Funds
- ETFs
- Variable Annuities

INVESTigator

INVESTigator compiles research of almost 30,000 individual companies (including public, private and corporate bonds).

- Biblically Responsible Screening
- Access Real-time Research
- Find Clean Alternatives
- U.S. Traded and International Stocks
- Private Companies

18

The Growing Movement

Therefore, since we are surrounded by such a great cloud of witnesses, let us throw off everything that hinders and the sin that so easily entangles. And let us run with perseverance the race marked out for us. —Hebrews 12:1

Being Invested with Purpose can feel like a lonely journey, whether we're doing it in our vocation, our business or in how we manage our money. There are times when we'll feel alone, but we need to remember that we're never alone. There is hope in knowing we have God the Father, the Son, and the Holy Spirit if we simply ask. If we search hard enough, we'll find others as convicted as we are, and our enthusiasm will inspire more to join us.

As Timothy Plan matured, others joined the movement. In December 1997, Art announced the formation of the National Association of Christian Financial Consultants (NACFC) to provide a forum for Christian advisors to come together, worship and figure out how to change investors' ideas about investing. Art served as president from 1998 to 2001. In 2005, the Association created the Christian Financial Consultant and Advisor (CFCA®) certification training program.

In 1997, Larry Burkett brought together 16 friends and professionals to form the Christian Financial Planning Institute (CFPI). These men and women created a new organization in 2003 for outreach to the Christian financial professional community. The Christian Financial Professionals Network (CFPN) under the leadership of Ron Blue began to grow, and in 2007 was re-named Kingdom Advisors.[1]

Former Templeton global portfolio manager and analyst Howard "Rusty" Leonard founded Stewardship Partners in 2000, and began managing money in separately managed accounts (SMAs) from a Christian worldview perspective.[2] While still at Templeton, Mr. Leonard and his wife Carol developed Wall Watchers, a ministry designed to help Christians be better stewards of their giving.

"SMAs differ from pooled vehicles like mutual funds in that each portfolio is unique to a single account (hence the name). If you set up a separate account with Money Manager X, Manager X has the discretion to make decisions for this account that may be different from decisions made for other accounts."[3]

Timothy Plan absorbed The Noah Fund, in 2005, which was founded in 1996 as a mutual fund based on Judeo-Christian principles and which invested only in "what we believe is a moral, spiritual and ethical standard, but also with an emphasis on low risk, high growth stocks."[4] The Fund tithed 10 percent of management earnings to "missions and the needs of the poor."[5]

A large Catholic firm, Ave Maria funds, was launched in 2001. "The fund's managers generally adhere to a socially conservative bent that excludes companies involved with abortion, contraception or pornography, as well as companies that offer domestic partner benefits."[6]

In 2012, the Christian Investment Forum (CIF), was formed[7] in Charlotte, N.C., as a "Kingdom-focused investment association committed to educating advisors and investors by providing opportunities to bring about change—in the hearts, homes, cities, nation, and world that we serve."[8] The CIF has 11 member firms (although each has its own unique screening criteria): Advisor Solutions 360, Beacon Wealth, Envoy Financial, Epiphany Funds, Eventide, Guidestone, In His Steps (IHS) Foundation, Praxis Mutual Funds, Sage Stone Wealth Management, Signatry, Timothy Plan, and Veriti.[9]

Other faith-based mutual funds reflect the values of Baptist, Lutheran, Presbyterian, Mennonite, and evangelical denominations. "The largest group in terms of assets is Guidestone Funds, which has more than $7 billion in assets spread across 23 funds, including five target-date funds," Forbes reports.[10] Guidestone avoids investing in companies that are publicly perceived to be involved in alcohol, tobacco, gambling, pornography, or abortion.

The Rise of Biblically Responsible Financial Advisors

As the field grew, more Christian financial advisors began screening for biblically sound investments. Some offered a stewardship-based approach even before the advent of Biblically Responsible Investing screening tools.

In Kokomo, Indiana, Mick L. Owens, who began his career in financial services in 1969, founded the Creative Financial Centre that year with a network of associates "committed to serving clients in a Christ-like manner by assisting them in development of stewardship in their lives."[11]

Among the most prominent BRI pioneer advisors was Glenn A. Repple of Florida-based G.A. Repple & Company, which is an Independent Financial Planning firm operating under the principles of Biblically Responsible Investing. Mr. Repple is a Certified Teacher of Biblical Entrepreneurship and has trained more than 600 business leaders who likewise have spread the BRI principles in 23 different countries.[12]

Others include Daniel L. Hardt of Dan Hardt Financial Services in Louisville, Kentucky, who, as president at one time of the National Association of Christian Financial Consultants, popularized the phrase "Biblically Responsible Investing" in his public speaking. [13]

Mark Minnella is another prominent figure in the BRI movement. In 2002, he founded Integrity Investors, L.L.C., a St. Louis-based company to align his clients' investments with their biblical beliefs. A co-founder of the National Association of Christian Financial Consultants, Inc., Mark designed the first biblically responsible professional designation program, Christian Financial Consultant and Advisor (CFCA®) and served at one time on the Timothy Plan Board of Trustees.

Comparable Returns

The primary purpose of Biblically Responsible Investing is to honor God by aligning the fund holders' values with their investments. A considerable body of research indicates investors do not have to hurt their bottom lines while doing so and may even reap higher returns in some cases.

A University of Pennsylvania's Wharton School of Business study in 2016 found that screened investments performed favorably against unscreened investment funds: "Impact funds in the sample that seek market-rate-returns demonstrate that they can achieve results comparable to market indices, while still reporting mission preservation in the vast majority of their exited investments."[14]

The study, "Great Expectations: Mission Preservation and Financial Performance in Impact Investing," said, "Market-rate-seeking impact investments in the sample, therefore, may be financially competitive on a gross basis with other equity investing investment opportunities. This financial performance may be why impact fund managers often assert that there is little inherent tension between profits and purpose."[15]

A 2014 meta-analysis of 85 studies and 190 experiments reported in Business Ethics: A European Review, found "consideration of corporate social responsibility in stock market portfolios is neither a weakness nor a strength compared with conventional investments."[16]

An Oxford University 18-year study of screened funds comprising 180 U.S. companies for "sustainability" and other factors such as excluding firms employing child labor, showed better returns, including lower cost of capital and "stock price performance."[17] The authors concluded "High Sustainability companies significantly outperform their counterparts over the long-term, both in terms of stock market as well as accounting."[18]

In 2015, a Christian Investment Forum study noted previous studies had established that Socially Responsible Investing, of which BRI is a subcategory, performed as well or better than unscreened funds.

In an effort to determine whether the smaller universe of BRI funds matched the overall SRI finding, the authors concluded, "Based on the analysis of historical performance data from the funds managed by members of the Christian Investment Forum [of which Timothy Plan is a participant], the results did in fact corroborate the expectation that return performance was not reduced due to incorporating BRI, and in fact there was a general outperformance compared to the industry averages."[19]

"Over the last 5 years, a composite of the returns from all of the equity mutual funds within the Christian Investment Forum outperformed the industry average by 77 basis points (bp) on an annualized basis."[20]

The author cautioned, "the results of this analysis are not meant to suggest that BRI funds will result in outperformance. The most important reason to incorporate BRI funds into an overall investment portfolio is to better align investments with an investor's values."[21]

Investors and advisors can have peace of mind "considering funds that can align with their Christian faith need not be a choice between values and performance."[22]

Impact Beyond Money

"Every day, people comment on how grateful they are and how blessed they are to have peace of mind their money is invested in areas that are not grieving the heart of God," says economist and radio commentator Dan Celia. "For the first time in many of their lives, they are not worried about money. They know God will honor their commitment."[23]

Mr. Celia has little patience with advisors trying to steer clients away from BRI-focused portfolios.

"If a financial advisor tries to talk you out of it, fire him (or her)," he said. "Advisors shouldn't question someone's convictions. They should be helping their clients fulfill their goals and their objective of being responsible with God's money. If they don't find an advisor who can help them do this, they should keep looking."[24]

Shane Enete, assistant professor of finance at Biola University, summarizes: "When a BRI product helps a Christian take seriously their role as steward of God's money through a combination of divesting, engaging and endorsing, that BRI product is serving the investor in a very meaningful way."[25]

The immediate positive impact is on the Christian investor, who no longer worries his or her dollars are funding immoral activities, and still receives a solid return on investment. Society also benefits, as companies take notice that many of their shareholders don't want their investments aiding anti-family, anti-marriage and anti-morality causes.

Finally, it's even good for financial advisors.

"As people become convicted of being biblically responsible investors, they are the best clients to have," Mr. Celia says. "They are at peace; they're not going to call every time the market goes down or become ecstatic when the market goes up. After 30 years of dealing with clients, I can say these are the best clients an advisor can have."[26]

The Master's Plan

As 403b retirement plans increased in regulations and fees—affordability decreased, and it became especially difficult for individual pastors or small churches to afford administration costs. Realizing the need, in 2017, Art—the rifter—mobilized yet another good idea by starting The Master's Plan and fulfilling his original dream to serve pastors in this capacity.

The Master's Plan is a low cost, Third Party Administrator (TPA). It provides services to biblically responsible 403b plans for churches and other non-ERISA Christian schools and 501c3 ministries with fewer than 100 participating employees.

These plans are limited to Timothy Plan investments. There are no administrative fees. Participants only pay an annual custodial fee of $10/year, which is paid to the custodian of the plan.

For more information, visit themastersplan.com.

Approaching Employers

What about Christian employees at secular companies with company-sponsored retirement plans? What should they do if their investment options amount only to a few mutual funds which include "sin stocks?"

"There's nothing wrong with bringing your employer's attention to the possibility of adding some investment choices incorporating BRI," said Mark Minnella. "First, Christian employees should be thankful and approach the employer with respect and thanksgiving for what they are doing. They could then point out that their current 401(k) includes an environmentally friendly fund—because most do—and they could say: 'That's great. We wonder if you would consider also doing this for those of us interested in BRI?'"[27]

Mr. Minnella also recommends downloading a letter provided by the screening site eVALUEator.com and sending it to the employer. "You could even send it anonymously, if you're worried about being singled out," he said.

> Are you feeling alone on this journey? Who else can you identify and encourage to join you? As the African proverb goes, if you want to go fast, go alone, but if you want to go far, go together. Find other like-minded people with whom you can share the journey.

Always remember before investing, consider each funds' investment objectives, risks, charges and expenses. A prospectus containing this information is available through your Financial Advisor or funds' website. Please read it carefully.

---

[1] Kingdom Advisors history at kingdomadvisors.com/about/history.

[2] "Our History," Stewardship Partners, at stewardshippartners.com/about.htm.

[3] Katrina Lamb, "Separately Managed Accounts: a Mutual Fund Alternative," Investopedia, updated January 24, 2018, at investopedia.com/articles/mutualfund/08/ managed-separate-account. asp.

[4] The Noah Fund, Internet Archive Wayback Machine, at noahfund.com:80.

[5] Ibid.

[6] David K. Randall, "Easy Ways to Invest Based on Your Faith," Forbes, May 22, 2009, at forbes. com/2009/05/22/faith-mutual-funds-moneybuilder-personal-finance-religious-investing.html#35ed16558844.

[7] CIF Facebook page, at facebook. com/pg/christianinvestmentforum/ about/?ref=page_internal.

[8] Christian Investment Forum home page at christianinvestmentforum.org.

[9] Ibid.

[10] Ibid.

[11] CFC Web page at cfcadvisers.com/about/mission and www.cfcadvisers.com/team/mick-l-owens-cfp.

[12] G.A. Repple web page at garepple. com/about.

[13] Telephone interview by Robert Knight on March 20, 2018.

[14] Jacob Gray, et al., "Great Expectations: Mission Preservation and Financial Performance in

Impact Investing," Wharton School of Business, University of Pennsylvania, p. 28, at socialimpact. wharton.upenn.edu/wp-content/uploads/2016/09/Great-Expectations-Mission-Preservation-and-Financial-Performance-in-Impact-Investing.pdf.

[15] Ibid, p. 27.

[16] Christophe Revelli and Jean-Laurent Viviani, "Financial performance of socially responsible investing (SRI): what have we learned? A meta-analysis," Business Ethics: A European Review, Vol. 24, Issue 2, April 2015, p 158, at onlinelibrary.wiley.com/doi/10.1111/beer.12076/abstract.

[17] Robert G. Eccles, Ioannis Ioannou, and George Serafeim, "The Impact of Corporate Sustainability on Organizational Processes and Performance," Smith School of Enterprise and the Environment, Oxford University, 2010, at hbs.edu/faculty/Publication%20Files/SSRN-id1964011_6791edac-7daa-4603-a220-4a0c6c7a3f7a.pdf.

[18] Ibid, p. 1.

[19] John Silverling, "A Research Study on CIF Member Funds Composite Performance Relative to Industry Averages," Christian Investment Forum White Paper, May 2015, p. 2, at christianinvestmentforum.org/content/uploads/2015/06/CIF-Study-on-BRI-Funds-Performance-Spring-2015.pdf.

[20] Ibid, p. 2.

[21] Ibid, p. 3.

[22] Ibid.

[23] Telephone interview with Dan Celia January 26, 2018.

[24] Ibid.

[25] Enete, "Inspired Investing: An introduction to Biblically Responsible Investing," Crowell School of Business, Biola University, at inspireinvesting.com/wp-content/uploads/2017/06/Inspired-Investing_Intro-To-Biblically-Responsible-Investing.pdf.

[26] Telephone interview with Dan Celia, January 26, 2018.

[27] Telephone interview with Mark Minnella, Jan. 26, 2018.

19

All in the Family

For I have chosen him, so that he will direct his children and his household after him to keep the way of the LORD by doing what is right and just.—Genesis 18:19a

One of the signs we're truly Invested with Purpose is our ability to rally our family around what God has called us to do. God doesn't call only individuals but often families. Make sure you give ample opportunity for your family to join you on your impact journey.

The Timothy Partners staff in its first two years consisted of Art, Bonnie, their son Steve, daughter Cheryl, attorney Terry Covert, and Geoffrey Murvin, who is since deceased.

Bonnie is office manager and has been with the firm since its inception. She coined the name Timothy Plan based on Bible verses from the book of I Timothy.

Steve is Chief Operating Officer, and earned a Bachelor of Arts degree in marketing and advertising from the University of Kentucky. He worked as the director of investment at Covenant Financial Management, which Art started as a boutique division of Investment Management & Research, a division of Raymond James. Shortly after launching Timothy Plan, Art needed Steve to join the team, so they sold the practice to a colleague and Steve joined the firm shortly after its inception in 1994.

Cheryl Ally Mumbert earned a Bachelor of Arts degree in education from the University of Central Florida. As Chief Marketing Officer, she manages the brand—including all marketing materials, data analytics, graphics, and quality control. She has been with the firm since its inception.

Art and Bonnie's eldest son, Douglas, was hired to manage ICS-RI, the firm conducting the screening research for Timothy Plan and eVALUEator. For over 21 years, Doug operated computers and technology in the Navy. These skills have proved to be invaluable with ICSRI. In 2018, Doug's wife Glenda joined ICSRI as a research specialist. Others serving on the ICSRI team include Beth Nelson and Belinda Ford.

An "Intimidating" Proposal

Cheryl's husband, Brian Mumbert, is Vice President of Financial Advisor Relations, supporting financial advisors who specialize in Biblically Responsible Investing in the Southern states and on the West Coast.

He met Cheryl when he came to work for the firm. "Having to ask for the hand of the boss's daughter was intimidating," he said. "Art knew my family and me from church, which helped a lot. Upon being hired, Art introduced me around the office. When we stopped by Cheryl's office, he introduced her as his 'still single daughter.'

"After working here for about one year, I pursued dating Cheryl. She was not exactly an easy person to convince to go out on a date. She was preoccupied with entertaining contenders from her eHarmony matches. I decided the best way to get to know each other was to suffer through hearing about her dating experiences. I offered my advice, which she rarely took.

"Eventually, the friendship grew, and she finally agreed to go out with me. Seeing how she was the boss's daughter, and the office had only 10 employees, this was not something I could do without notice."

Mustering up all the courage he had, Brian went to Art and asked for permission to date his daughter.

"It was very much like a marriage proposal," Brian said. "Art is quite an intimidating person, and he quickly informed me that if the relationship did not end well, it would undoubtedly be my job and not Cheryl's that would be on the line.

"It didn't end there. Cheryl still lived at home with her parents. On one of our first dates, I rang the doorbell, and Art answered the door. He curtly asked me what I was doing there and then slammed the door. He let me sweat for about 30 seconds and then invited me in. It was one of his typical gags."

When it came time for an actual proposal, Brian related, "There isn't much more there—the hard part was the initial part. He did give Cheryl what he called 'almost an unlimited budget' for our wedding in 2007, which he often clarifies she managed to exceed."

Brian's brother, Stephen Mumbert, was hired in March 2015, and serves on the shareholder services team. In addition to his secu-

rities licenses, Stephen earned a Bachelor of Music in vocal performance from Stetson University and a Master of Music in opera
from The Boston Conservatory. He has performed throughout the
United States and Europe.

Stephen's wife, Shannon Mumbert, is the Executive Administrative Assistant to Art Ally and Terry Covert. Before joining the firm
in 2017, Shannon worked for 17 years at a major financial institu-
tion. She brings a wealth of experience to the team.

Competitors to Colleagues

Terry Covert came aboard in February 1995. "Art invited me in
November, and I had three job offers. He came to me in January,
and he said, 'I guess you don't want to join us.' I told him, 'God
hasn't talked to me yet.'"

At that time, Terry had to have eye surgery. "Art and Bonnie were
the only ones who came to see how I did." During a quiet time, Terry heard God's call for him to join the firm. He called Art and said,
"God told me to come to work for you."

"My wife Sandy and I had been friends with Art and Bonnie since
1979," Terry said. "We were friendly competitors the first 10 years
we knew each other. He was with Bache Halsey Stuart Shields, and
I was with Paine Webber, and we were attending the same church—
Winter Park Christian Church. Doug was 16, Steve 14, and Cheryl 8
when we met. Art had a knack for moving all over the country. We
visited the Ally family at each home over the years."

Terry, who is Chief Compliance Officer and in-house legal counsel,
is jokingly referred to as "Dr. No." Terry's job is to make sure Timothy
Plan and Timothy Partners are in full compliance with the U.S. Securities and Exchange Commission (SEC) and FINRA. Among other

things, Terry reviews copious marketing materials.

His son, Zachary Covert, who previously ran his own digital and telemarketing company, came aboard in 2017. Zachary serves as the Director of Advisor Relations for the Northeast and Midwest.

The Harts' Part

In 1999, Art hired Dave Hart to help market Timothy Plan. "He is the greatest salesman I have ever met in my life," Art said. Dave is now running eVALUEator.

Dave's wife, Debbie Hart, is Vice President of Investor Relations. Debbie joined the team in 2000. She had been a surety bond under-writer for Old Republic Surety and then later with Hartford Insur-ance Company. "We provided surety bonds for contractors, small businesses, etc.," she said.

"Shortly after starting, the market was a mess," Debbie said. "I asked Art if I should put my resume out, but he told me to hang in there."

2000: FROM LEFT, DAVE HART, STEVE ALLY, DEBBIE HART, TERRY COVERT, BONNIE ALLY, ART ALLY, CHERYL ALLY

Art has a reputation for taking care of his people. Debbie remembered, "When my Dad was dy-ing around Christmas time, Art told us 'You're evicted. You and Dave are out of the office until this happens.'"

In 2008, when the economy tanked along with the stock market, Art brought everyone into the conference room and asked if any employees would voluntarily reduce their salaries to avoid laying off anyone. "Nearly everyone stepped up and sacrificed," Art recalls.

"No one was let go, even though most firms were laying off people," Debbie recalled.

Dave's sister, Barbara Catoe, is Trade Coordinator and has worked at the office since 2004. Along with tracking and reconciling all sub-advisor trades coming through Timothy Plan. Barbara supports the team with office and administration duties.

The Staff Keeps Growing

Over the years, more family members of staff were added, and the office now resembles a large, extended family. Even non-family members feel like family.

Robin Bryant earned a Bachelors of Science in business law from the University of Central Florida and in 2007 was hired as Executive Administrative Assistant to Art Ally and Terry Covert. In 2018, she transitioned to supporting The Master's Plan, a newly formed retirement plan TPA. She is an Associate Retirement Specialist working with Retirement Specialist Barbara A. Hanis.

Robin's husband, David Bryant, is Director of Investor Relations and previously served the Northeast region of Advisor Relations. He joined in 2007. "One of the perks working for Art is there is always great food. Food is Art's love language," said David. "There's nearly always something delicious in the kitchen."

In 2007, Nick Butler came aboard as Technology Director supporting the firm and all of its affiliated entities.

Kim Billips joined in 2017 as Director of Creative Marketing after spending 23 years as a marketing director in the architectural field. She works closely with Cheryl to ensure Timothy Plan's "look" is bright, imaginative, and consistent in all of its products and publications.

In 2017, Cara Groenendaal joined as an associate in creative communications. She has 10 years of experience working in hospitality for five-star resorts and is advancing her knowledge in digital media.

Cindy Best is Director of Advisor Relations for the East region and joined the firm in 2018. With more than 20 years of experience in the financial investment arena, she has partnered with advisors nationwide to help build their BRI practices.

Melissa Rhodes is the newest team member providing support to the wholesaling department.

Learning to "Chill"

At one time, Liberty Counsel occupied the second floor suite of the same building where Timothy Plan is located. Robin recalls running into Art in an elevator one day as she was in the process of leaving her position at Liberty Counsel. Art asked her to come to work for him.

After accepting the position as Executive Assistant, Robin said, "Art asked me to come to his office. I had nothing to do for my first couple of weeks. I sat around all day and did nothing. I answered the phone once, and he shook his head. After some time he finally asked, 'Are you ready to come to work here now?' He was conditioning me to chill." It worked. After the season of learning to chill, Art kept her very busy.

The hiring culture is unique at Timothy Partners. As Colleen Barrett, former Southwest Airlines president said, "We hire for attitude and train for skill." We are a Christian professional service company with a commitment to excellence to our shareholders.

The Next Generation

"My father has softened over the years, while still having 'his moments,' said Cheryl. "I guess those moments are bound to happen over the twenty-five years of working together. It is understood I am not allowed to 'permanently' quit or be fired—although it temporarily happens. As family, we are bonded together. This became abundantly clear when a miracle happened, and I became pregnant against many odds.

"I had Noah at the age of 39. The doctors did their best to scare Brian and me into having tests done that could actually harm our baby, just to make sure he was 'normal, by their standards.' We chose to skip those awful tests and trusted God for any outcome because He knows what he is doing. Right then, I pledged to God, if my son made it into this world, he would be His warrior.

"God did not choose 'normal' for my son. It is impossible to take credit for his extraordinarily sweet, polite, and forgiving nature. If you met him, you would know this to be true. God is good!

"After a few months of maternity leave, Art (aka Dad) allowed me to bring my son to work until he was almost one. Art wanted me to be at the office—I thought I wanted to be a stay at home mom. The office needed me, my family needed me, and my son needed me—the balancing act was a struggle every working mom understands. For the first few years I worked from home, which was a blessing.

"Art wanted me back at the office. Although I was ready to come back, I did not want Noah to be raised through a daycare system. Art understood this and did what he could to support my wishes. I was blessed to have family and friends watching Noah before he started school and was thankful to spend time with him at the office after school.

"Now almost ten, Noah still enjoys coming to the office after school. He thinks he works here and loves it. Through this support from my dad, Noah has become a grandchild to those who do not have any, and is loved by everyone—even the postman."

When Noah was asked what he plans to be when he grows up, his answer was, "I want to be just like my grandfather."

Cheryl designed the book cover to capture Timothy Plan's past and future, a 1994 penny held by Art's grandson, Noah.

"Thank you for your legacy, Dad." –Cheryl Marie

> Have you been able to inspire your family to come alongside your vision? Remember, God calls not only individuals, but also families. Do your part to encourage your family to join you, so together you can impact your community and the kingdom of God for His glory.

Faith-Driven Activism

Before I formed you in the womb I knew you, before you were born I set you apart; I appointed you as a prophet to the nations.—Jeremiah 1:5

> You cannot be Invested with Purpose without a commitment to the unborn. The Bible is clear that life begins not just at birth. God knew us before we were born. Our births were not accidental, but rather, intentional acts of God with His purpose for us to realize on the earth. Being Invested with Purpose is not our design but God's original plan for us.

Art was pro-life for as long as he can remember, yet it was when he and Bonnie attended a screening of "Silent Scream" that he really woke to the horrors of abortion and decided to do something about it.

"The movie was life changing for both Bonnie and me," Art said. "Once you come to grips with what abortion really is, you simply cannot continue to stand on the sidelines. Not only that, but as Bible-believing Christians who were beginning to fully understand God is Creator and Finisher of all life, to simply sit back and do nothing was not an option."

Art became active in Florida's pro-life movement and served in a leadership role in numerous pro-life rallies and events during the late 1980s up through today.

His activism began while living in Boca Raton, and his first real involvement was a rally called Why We Stand. Held in the fall of 1987, it drew thousands of people and featured numerous national pro-life speakers, including Josh McDowell and several elected officials. This rally served to fuel Art's un-

Baptist layman organizes Orlando pro-life rally

By Patricia Bolen
Special to the Witness

Central Florida Christians concerned about abortion will gather at a pro-life rally Saturday, March 3, from 10 a.m. to noon at Lake Eola Park in downtown Orlando.

Art Ally, a layman in First Church of Winter Park, is spearheading the effort, which he hopes will draw 3,000 people from the Central Florida area.

"It's not a Baptist rally, but a Christian rally," said Ally, chairman of the Rally for Life committee planning the event. "Although Baptists have taken leadership posts, we've invited other denominations to be involved. The 49 members of our committee represent 15 or 16 congregations from eight or nine denominations."

Keynote speaker for the rally will be Mildred Jefferson, a leading crusader in the pro-life cause. She was the first black woman to graduate from Harvard University with a doctorate. She currently is running for a Senate seat from Massachusetts.

The agenda includes former state convention president Bobby Welch, pastor of First Church of Daytona Beach, who will challenge Christians to become involved in the pro-life movement. The program also features testimonies, skits and a 250-voice choir.

To organize the rally, Ally formed a network of concerned Christians and churches. A survey identified 250 churches in the Central Florida area with pro-life convictions. Each of those churches was asked to appoint a representative to serve as a liaison between the church and the Rally for Life committee. "I believe our key to success is the liaison network," Ally said.

In addition to the March 3 rally in Orlando, organizers are asking church members to attend an April 17 rally in Tallahassee, which coincides with the opening of the Florida state legislature. They also are encouraging pro-life Christians to register to vote and go to the polls in September and November.

At the rally, tables will be set up for voter registration for Orange County residents. There also will be information booths to provide background and support material.

Ally, who is vice president of an investment firm, served on a pro-life committee in Boca Raton before moving to Orlando. "The education and awareness that came out of the Boca rally touched me," he said. "I want to share that here."

He encourages Baptists throughout the state to plan rallies similar to the March 3 event in their areas.

Ally explains his motivation for involvement in the pro-life movement: "When history is written about the time period in which we live, I don't want it to ask the question, 'Where was the church?' And, when I meet the Lord, I want to have an answer when he asks, 'Where were you?'

"The word 'enough' symbolizes my feelings," he continued. "It's time for Christians to stand up and say, 'enough; this is wrong,' and put their beliefs on the line."

J. C. Mitchell, Florida Baptist State Convention president and Ally's pastor, said: "The abortion crisis is the burning issue in America today. It is most encouraging that laymen are giving leadership to reversing this holocaust in our society. Because of his deep conviction, Art Ally has given himself unreservedly to the cause of saving unborn babies from death. His leadership with others is infectious."

Mitchell calls summit of religious leaders to address abortion

J. C. Mitchell, president of the Florida Baptist State Convention, has called a summit of religious leaders to develop a pro-life strategy for the state.

Ken Conner, president of the Florida Right to Life, will give a brief talk and then there will be a question-and-answer period.

The meeting is scheduled for 11 a.m. Feb. 26 at the Radisson Plaza Hotel in Orlando.

wavering passion for the protection of the lives of the unborn.

On January 15, 1988, the Palm Beach Post reported that in conjunction with the upcoming rally, Art and 13 other businessmen and women "vowed to offer indigent pregnant women in Boca Raton a choice: If they reject abortion and choose life, they would help pay the cost of raising those children for 18 years."

After returning to Central Florida, Art decided to duplicate the Boca Raton rally by holding one in Orlando on February 22, 1990.

"As far as I knew, this was one of the first pro-life rallies in Cen-

tral Florida," Art said. "Once again, we had a lineup of speakers, including syndicated columnist Cal Thomas, that drew a crowd of several thousand."

Then Art, along with other Central Florida pro-life leaders, heard about a Life Chain event in Bakersfield, California, where pro-life advocates lined major streets holding signs reading "Abortion Kills Children."

"We decided we should do one here in Central Florida," Art said.

"They decided I should lead it. We held organizational meetings for several months, leading up to Orlando's first Life Chain on October 6, 1991. With the help of willing churches, we had 9,000 Central Floridians standing, side by side, lining two of the busiest streets in Orlando, holding signs. One read 'Abortion Kills Children,' and the other read 'Jesus Heals and Forgives.'

"At that time, it was one of the largest life chains in the country. With an understanding of media bias on this issue before the event, we met with the Orlando Sentinel editor and explained to him we didn't want the same thing to happen here that happened in Fresno, California. There, the Fresno Bee over-reported the size of a small group of pro-abortion demonstrators and far underreported the number of people standing in the life chain. This led to a boy-

cott of their newspaper by tens of thousands of subscribers. As a result, we received fair coverage for our Orlando event. They got the message."

"We repeated the event the following year, and working with willing churches, we ended up with more than 10,000 participants lining the streets for two hours. The next year, my last year as chairman, we gathered again, this time growing to over 15,000 participants. It took your breath away when you were driving down either of the two streets. This one was reported to be the strongest turnout in the nation."

That year, nationally, 700,000 participants in 360 cities lined intersections, making 1991 an historical declaration of support for the unborn.

"In 2003, we met with all the crisis pregnancy leaders in Central Florida and heard their thoughts on Timothy Plan's distributor sponsoring a pro-life concert to raise money for them," Art said. "Of course, they became excited. In October, Debbie Hart, an outstanding vocalist in her own right, recruited other top vocalists. The event was so successful we hosted more concerts over the next three years."

Many crisis pregnancy centers benefited, including Adoption by Shepherd Care, Greater Orlando Right to Life, JMJ Life Center, Inc., Pro-Life Action Ministries, Sanctuary Ministries, Life for Kids, and True Life Choice.

"More recent events include buying out a theater to show the movie 'Gosnell' to our local community in 2018," Art said. "On March 26, 2019, we bought out seven theaters in a 20-theater complex to show the movie 'Unplanned.'

"It was a real hit since these 500 'free' tickets paid for by Timothy Plan's distributor were snapped up within 24 hours. At the movie's conclusion, we asked the audience to remain for a couple of minutes while we introduced the directors of eleven of our local pro-life, crisis pregnancy centers."

Art promises, "We will continue to support pro-life ministries, as well as other causes advancing biblical principles."

Are you convicted about protecting the unborn? What can you do to ensure that every child not only lives but also gets a chance to realize God's intended purpose for him or her? No child is an accident. No matter the circumstances of anyone's birth, God is in complete control.

21

Reclaiming Our States

And you will be my witnesses in Jerusalem, and in all
Judea and Samaria, and to the ends of the earth.
—Acts 1:8b

> The impact we make while being Invested with Purpose
> must start in our own backyard. If each of us makes a
> commitment first to our own Jerusalem, as Jesus in-
> structed, before long, we will see a great difference in our
> nation. The change we are looking for will not be found
> in Washington, D.C., but in communities across America.
> As we change our communities, it will lead to change in
> Washington. Let's all start in our own Jerusalem.

A few years ago, a new force emerged whose ambition is to ac-
tivate a sleeping giant—millions of Christians who are politically

uninvolved, but who could make a difference in their communities and government. I have had the privilege of being part of Reclaiming Florida for Christ since its incubation.

When President Obama won his second term in 2012, there appeared to be a shift in our country, popularizing socialism and secularism. I thought, maybe now, pastors would be motivated to do what they should have been doing all along, which is to contend for our culture. Pastors, broadly speaking, seem disengaged in the cultural war.

Mobilizing Grass Roots

We assembled a team of nationally-renowned speakers, loaded into an RV, and started barnstorming Florida from Pensacola to Miami and from Jacksonville to Naples. We hosted breakfasts, lunches, and dinners in various cities for pastors and their wives.

Our objective was to seek out pastors who embraced the vision, understanding that the majority would not. With the support of several nationally respected speakers (*see list), we explained our cultural problems to church leaders. We traveled the state in an RV, and because of this barnstorming tour, we were able to identify about 500 pastors who 'got it.' We know there are many more, we just didn't find them all yet.

Drawing from Nehemiah

We tried to stay in touch with them; however, we were understaffed for proper follow-through. In 2014 and 2015, we changed gears and did another barnstorming tour across Florida every weekend from April to October.

This tour was aimed at building a volunteer army of precinct workers based on the principles outlined in the Book of Nehemiah. Our goal was to locate between three and five volunteers in every precinct in Florida who would be concerned with only their "section of the wall," so to speak, i.e., their precinct. Their objective was to knock on every door in their precinct and do a brief, three-question survey:

1) *Do you consider yourself pro-life or pro-choice?*
2) *Do you think we need more gun control in America?*
3) *Do you actively attend a church or synagogue?*

If the latter answer was no, they'd ask:

4) *Would you consider receiving an invitation to attend one?*

They would politely thank those who opposed conservative views and moved on to concentrate on the conservatives.

Their purpose was to support voter registration and encourage conservatives to vote their values. We introduced them to iVoterGuide as a resource on how to do both. From the website they can find instructions on voter registration, view their exact ballot, view research various candidates and their positions, along with an iVoterGuide rating from very conservative to very liberal.

We ended up identifying about 3,500 precinct volunteers over these two years. It was a good start, but, again, the initiative stumbled on follow-up. Our third push resulted from an event Richard Ford, founder of iVoterGuide, insisted I attend in Dallas, Texas, in 2016. Although I hesitated, he insisted, so I went. The event drew about 150 local Christian business owners and CEOs along with several conservative elected officials.

The purpose of the meeting was to encourage Christian CEOs and business owners to support their elected officials when they stand for righteousness. Too often, officials who do this find themselves standing alone. I was there to just observe, but when I saw the expressions on the faces of those Christian CEOs and business owners, I knew they understood.

Bringing It Home

I thought to myself, 'surely we can do this in Orlando.' We scheduled our event at the end of 2016 at the Orlando Country Club and started issuing invitations to Christian business owners and CEOs. Since we didn't know all of them, we engaged conveners who extended the invitations. I assembled a speaking slate of eleven outstanding Christian leaders from around the country for this call to action.

We drew about 125 participants, and the enthusiastic feedback I received was unprecedented. However, I started thinking this would not have broad impact unless we do this in every city in the state of Florida.

We organized another tour with the same group of speakers—these were three-hour events. We scheduled breakfast in Tallahassee, lunch in Jacksonville, breakfast in Daytona, and lunch in Ocala. The response was as encouraging as in Orlando, so we decided to keep going. A few months later, we slated another tour through Lakeland, Tampa, Fort Myers, and Sarasota. We were pleased to receive the same level of excitement as the others.

We still have not taken a tour to the East Coast of Florida, but we aim to cover Melbourne, Stuart, West Palm Beach, and Fort Lauderdale. Our follow-up to all of these includes recruiting a leader in each city who would serve on our statewide board of directors.

Taking it a step further, I was convicted to start up a PAC (political action committee). With no idea of what I was doing, I located a law firm in Virginia with considerable expertise. We wanted to allow these business owners an opportunity to fund a PAC whose funds the board of directors would distribute among quality candidates running for office.

Reclaiming Florida

It was a bit confusing since we were dealing with pastors, precinct workers, and Christian business owners. We reconfigured the team to do some follow-up. It now has four members under the banner of Reclaiming Florida for Christ. Headed by Pastor Dexter Sanders, the team includes Jenay McPherson, Charlie Nelson, and Joyce Sepulveda.

This project is based on the three legged stool concept of encouraging pastors, business leaders, and precinct volunteers to be engaged with tools that will help change the hearts and minds of people in our state.

With that focus, the team is now able to address each of those areas individually. With the help of Paul Blair, we have hosted multiple day-and-a-half pastor "training camps" to support, equip, and provide networking for willing pastors. The attendees' excitement has been invigorating and has added momentum to the mission.

One of the problems in the church today is that there may be pastors willing to be involved but ill-equipped to engage this current culture from a biblical perspective. We're equipping them, providing resources, and continuing education under a Liberty Pastors Network. Now they're able to stand together under this informal network.

We believe this will be a game changer not only for the battle-ground state of Florida but throughout the United States as well.

> Are you currently involved in your own community? How is what you're doing impacting it? Remember, before going to the ends of the earth, we must start in our Jerusalem.

---

* The speaker rotation at the various events included:

Art Ally
President
Timothy Plan

Debbie Wuthnow
Executive Director
iVoterGuide

Lea Carawan
Executive Director
Congressional Prayer Caucus
Foundation

Bob Williamson
Founder/CEO
Jesus Alliance

Mat Staver
Founder and President
Liberty Counsel

Ken Eldred
Co-Founder/CEO
Living Stones Foundation

Randy Forbes
Retired Republican – VA
U.S. Representative

John Stemberger
President and General Counsel
Florida Family Policy Council

Alan Hays
Former Florida State Senator

Paul Blair
Pastor and Former NFL Player

Rick Scarborough
Founder
Vision America

Norm Miller
Chairman
Interstate Batteries

Ken Blackwell
Former Ohio Secretary of State

Janet Porter
Founder
Faith2Action

K. Carl Smith
Author
"Frederick Douglass Republicans"

Dran Reese
Founder and President
Salt & Light Council

Curtis Bowers
Director/Producer
"Agenda" and "Agenda 2"

With the list still growing

22

Giving Back

But store up for yourselves treasures in heaven, where moths and vermin do not destroy, and where thieves do not break in and steal. For where your treasure is, there your heart will be also.—Matthew 6:20-21

As we conclude our journey together, let's look at the value of giving back. Invested with Purpose is all about others, not us. It's about giving, not receiving. It's about flourishing so we may enable others to flourish. Here are some examples of how Timothy Plan, by achieving success through Biblically Responsible Investing, has enabled others to flourish.

Timothy Plan's distributor currently sponsors at least 30 ministries through its earnings.

The various organization supported are on the front lines to help the people of our great nation stay true to the vision of our founding fathers—to maintain a moral and supportive community, through ministries focusing on:

- Ending abortion with the support of legislation, pregnancy centers, and community outreach.
- Fighting for stricter laws and awareness of child labor and sex trafficking.
- Protecting the rights of Christians all over the world.
- Preparing biblical entrepreneurs as they enter the marketplace.
- Supporting family values in our culture's entertainment.

Some of the ministries include Nehemiah Project, Liberty Counsel, Faith2Action, Financial Issues Stewardship Ministries, Movieguide, Hope for Israel, House of Hope, Give Kids the World Village, Choices Women's Clinic, Orange County Jail Ministry, Florida Family Policy Council, Pro-Life Action Ministries, American Decency Association, Salt & Light Council, Florida Abolitionist, Women Impacting the Nation, Parents Television Council, Special Olympics, Back2God, and Vision America.

Nehemiah Project

NEHEMIAHPROJECT.ORG

Nehemiah Project was founded in 1999 by husband and wife Patrice and Gina Tsague in Washington D.C. with the help of Patrice's mother, the Mustard Seed Foundation, and Tyrone Grigsby. Through these relationships, the program was launched in Cameroon. In 2004, with the help of Dr. John Mulford of Regent University, Art Ally of Timothy Plan, and Glenn Repple of G.A. Repple and Company, Nehemiah began its national expansion while carrying on its reach all over the world.

Patrice and Gina both arrived in the United States in 1983, with Patrice coming from Cameroon, Central Africa, and Gina from Haiti. During their high school years, they met at work and soon became friends. Patrice started his own business at the age of 18 and invited his best friend and chief encourager, Gina, to join him in his new venture. Through a series of events, this initial business idea evolved into Nehemiah Project and Kingdom Business Coaching.

Nehemiah Project has trained over 20,000 entrepreneurs in 38 countries to become biblically responsible through the Biblical Entrepreneurship Training Program.

Liberty Counsel
LC.ORG

Best known as a Christian law firm fighting for religious freedom, Liberty Counsel is actually a multi-pronged, international ministry with offices in Orlando, Florida, Lynchburg, Virginia, and Washington, D.C.

Founded in 1989, and headed by Mat and Anita Staver, Liberty Counsel defends Christian civil liberties at the Supreme Court level and in other venues for constitutional law. Mat also serves on Timothy Plan's Board of Trustees.

In Washington, D.C., its Faith & Liberty office serves as a Christian outreach to top-level government officials. Its mission is "to affect the hearts and minds of America's public policymakers with Christ's mandate in the two Great Commandments: Love God With

All Your Heart, Soul, Mind and Strength, and Love Your Neighbor As Yourself."

Liberty Counsel also comprises:

- Liberty Church Council, the spiritual, theological, and doctrinal advisory body of LC;

- International litigation, education, and policy ministry;

- Liberty Counsel Action, a ministry focused on education and public policy;

- Liberty Prayer Network, a worldwide prayer ministry; and

- Liberty Relief International, an international humanitarian ministry to persecuted Christians and religious minorities.

Faith2Action

FAITH2ACTION.ORG

Launched in 2010 by pro-life activist Janet (Folger) Porter, Faith2Action is an Ohio-based umbrella group that facilitates actions by the entire pro-family movement.

Under Mrs. Porter's leadership, Faith2Action began and inspired campaigns to enact "heartbeat" laws in several states. On May 8, 2019, Georgia's governor signed the latest state law (at this writing) banning abortions once a heartbeat is detected (usually at six weeks). Ohio, Mississippi, and Kentucky also enacted heartbeat laws in 2019, preceded by laws enacted in Iowa (2018) and North Dakota (2013), both of which were struck down by judges. More states are considering heartbeat laws, which may trigger a future challenge at the Supreme Court to Roe v. Wade.

Faith2Action's key Bible verse is: "Faith by itself, if it is not accompanied by action, is dead." James 2:17 (NIV)

The group's website states that its mission is "Pro-Life, Pro-Family, Pro-ACTIVE."

"Whether you search by issue or by state, Faith2Action provides the largest network of pro-family organizations in which to enlist," says Mrs. Porter. "It's not about the uniforms we wear or the branch of the cultural war in which we're called; it's about combining our strengths and winning on the issues that matter most.

"Faith2Action is about being faithful where the battle is the hottest—where our Bible-based beliefs and freedoms are most at risk. But beyond defending the issues that are most under attack, Faith2Action is about advancing—taking back ground. Our goal isn't to just survive the cultural war, but to win it.

"Faith2Action provides pro-active, strategic, and unified ways to ADVANCE the cause of Christ and the kingdom of God. We are turning people of faith into people of action to WIN the cultural war together for life, liberty, and the family."

Financial Issues Stewardship Ministries
FINANCIALISSUES.ORG

This is the ministry of famed Christian financial advocate Daniel J. Celia, whose radio program is on over 640 stations three hours daily, plus NRB TV, BizTV, Dove TV and CBN Lifestyle Network. "Financial Issues" is heard in every state in America and throughout the internet globally.

In 1999, Dan sold his Small Trust Company (managing over $900 million) to go into ministry. He started a radio ministry in 1997 as a part-time ministry and has seen the Lord expand and bless this ministry to his current full-time ministry. Dan is now president,

CEO of Financial Issues Stewardship Ministries (FISM). Dan has developed a biblically responsible system of financial management with great success.

"After all, God does own all of it—not just what we give to Him, but He owns the rest as well," Dan says. "We are expected to be responsible in our investments. This ministry exists so that we can help investors make good decisions with what God has blessed them with. The idea is that if we can help investors to be comfortable in their investment strategies and decisions, then they will be more comfortable in their giving. Hopefully, they will also have more to give in the long run."

American Family Online (AFO)

AFO.NET

Founded in 1998 by Steve Ensley, AFO's provides the best and safest internet services available. Over the years, their products and services have expanded to multiple filtering technologies and internet services while keeping their focus on internet safety—protecting families from the "dark side" of the internet.

AFO has been hosting sites for Timothy Partners and Timothy Plan for over ten years and has been essential in developing its database driven websites. Steve and his team work closely with Nick and Cheryl.

Steve was significantly impacted by the Biblical Stewardship Series almost 20 years ago. He has been a huge advocate for the course and felt called to create an online version to make it available to everyone. After a few years of development, the course is now available at no cost at biblicalstewardshiponline.org.

Movieguide
MOVIEGUIDE.ORG

Founded in 1985 by Dr. Ted Baehr, Movieguide's mission is to redeem the values of the entertainment industry according to biblical principles by influencing industry executives and artists.

Movieguide reviews movies from a Christian perspective and how movies affect children at different stages of cognitive development. The staff analyzes movies using over 150 different criteria that cover the dramatic elements, the literary, the worldview, the theological, and more.

The ministry, which started in Atlanta and is now headquartered in Camarillo, California, launched a radio program, a TV program, a bi-weekly magazine and TV and radio shows in over 200 countries and a website filled with resources including movie reviews and articles.

Each year, Movieguide provides an annual report to the film industry, comparing average box office receipts against those with moral content—with often surprising findings. Films "with very strong non-Christian, false or immoral worldviews" average far less than films with more wholesome content.

In February 2018, at Movieguide's annual gala, Art Ally presented the Kairos Prize, awarded by the Christian Film & Television Commission for Spiritually Uplifting Screenplays, and also the Beginning Screenwriter award.

"It's our pleasure to encourage wholesome movie-making that can shine a light in an ever-coarser popular culture," Art said. "We'd rather light a candle than curse the darkness."

House of Hope

HOUSEOFHOPE.ORG

The House of Hope has been a beacon to troubled teens and their families since 1985, when Sara Trollinger started this remarkable youth outreach in Orlando.

A junior high school teacher for 25 years, Sara was also instructing at the juvenile detention center in Orange County, Florida. "The same teens would come and go," she recalls. "We could not even mention Jesus. It was like a revolving door."

Tired of watching kids ruin their lives with sex, drugs, and rebellion, she launched the Central Florida HOPE telephone ministry. "Almost all the calls were from distraught moms and teens," she says. Then, the Lord told her to start a residential program for girls, which became the House of Hope.

A non-denominational, not-for-profit, Christ-centered residential program, House of Hope "offers hurting teens, ages 13-17, a place to find hope and healing in a loving, supportive environment and be reconciled to their families."

In 2000, a National House of Hope opened, and Houses of Hope in several other cities became affiliated in 2002 with the Orlando facility as the model. Sara, who also serves on the board of the National Coalition Against Pornography, began traveling with Women of Faith, bringing along some teens who have benefited from House of Hope. The program also partners with the American Association for Christian Counselors.

Hope for Israel

HOPE4ISRAEL.ORG

Founded in 2000 by Moran Rosenblit, an Israeli Army veteran who had moved to California to make a new start in life and now lives in Israel, Hope for Israel has grown into a multi-level ministry offering biblical teaching, Gospel outreach, material aid to needy Jews and Arabs alike, and a wealth of information about modern Israel. Plus, they do an excellent job correcting much of the "fake news" about Israel.

"We love the Jewish people and we're told in Scripture that the Lord blesses those who bless Israel," said Timothy Plan founder and President Art Ally.

One of the reasons for launching the Timothy Plan Israel Common Values mutual fund seven years ago was to counter growing anti-Semitism in liberal circles and the BDS Movement (Boycott, Divestment, and Sanctions) against Israel on college campuses and in major cities.

Give Kids the World Village

GKTW.ORG

Not far from Disney World, there's a magical place where children with life-threatening illnesses can go into a cookie shop and walk out with delicious treats, or another shop where they can eat ice cream sundaes without limit.

They can play games at kiosks, or dance with Disney princesses and other Disney characters. And they can do all this at no expense. In fact, the children and their families can stay for free in one of more than 80 fancifully decorated suites on 84 acres when they are not tooling around Disney World or Epcot Center, again at no expense.

The families are guests at Give Kids the World Village, "a cross between Disney and Whoville," said Robin Bryant, which has proudly supported the Village for the past five years.

The brainchild of the late hotelier and philanthropist Henri Landwirth, a Holocaust survivor with a huge heart for children, the Village makes it possible for families that have children with life-threatening illnesses to enjoy a wondrous time at the world's most celebrated theme park.

The Village staff works closely with the Make-a-Wish foundation and other charities that help these children realize their dream.

Choices Women's Clinic

CHOICESMINISTRIES.ORG

For 36 years, Vicky Mathews and her staff have been assisting mothers (and fathers) to keep their babies instead of aborting them, a route she regrettably took many years ago. Helping others has been key to her own healing, she said.

Orlando has six abortion clinics, including four late-term clinics. CHOICES was planted in 1983 deliberately near three of them.

As the CHOICES website explains: "1 in 4 pregnancies in the U.S. ends in abortion. More than 11,000 of those abortions happen right here in the greater Orlando area. Choices Women's Clinic works to reach men and women in need to impact them for life and Christ. Orlando may be a fun place to live, work, and play, but the sad truth is that the lives of 35 babies are terminated every day at abortion clinics in our City Beautiful!

"Choices Women's Clinic's ministries all work together to save lives—not just those of the unborn, but the mothers that carry them. We find that when a baby's life is saved, it has a positive ripple effect across an entire family—and for generations to come."

Orange County Jail Ministry

Founded in 1980 in Orlando to bring inmates to the saving knowledge of Jesus Christ, Orange County Jail Ministry has seven chaplains, three assistants, and one office administrator, all while providing Bibles, study materials and many reading glasses to inmates.

In 2018, over 2,000 inmates received the gift of salvation, and throughout their stay, the ministry continues to nurture them in the principles of Christian living.

More than 300 volunteers including Art's son, Douglas, minister to the inmates and the governing board comprises volunteers from many denominations. The ministry is nonsectarian in recognition of the inmates' many religious affiliations.

Florida Family Policy Council

FLFAMILY.ORG

One of 38 state-based policy councils associated with Focus on the Family, the Florida Family Policy Council was founded in 2004.

A leading pro-life, pro-family organization, FFPC's motto is "For Life, Marriage, Family, and Liberty." Its Vision is "A Nation Where God is Honored, Life is Cherished, Families Thrive and Religious Liberty Flourishes."

John Stemberger is the group's founding President and remains the organization's CEO and General Counsel. He is also on the founding board of Trail Life USA, a growing alternative to the Boy Scouts of America.

Florida Family Policy Council "is committed to using good research, sound arguments, and articulate presentations to make a case for pro-life, pro-family values in the public square."

Pro-Life Action Ministries

PLAM.ORG

An interdenominational Christian organization dedicated to publicly defending the sanctity of human life, Pro-Life Action Ministries helps save lives from abortion, infanticide ,and euthanasia through peaceful direct-action and educational projects.

This ministry "began with a peaceful sit-in conducted on March 5, 1981, by four young adults (Michael Gaworski, Paul O'Donnell, Gary Gaworski and Bill Vouk) inside the Planned Parenthood abortion center in St. Paul, Minnesota. Since then, Pro-Life Action Ministries has been on the front lines of the abortion battle, working diligently to save the lives of God's precious little children each and every day, with the ultimate goal of helping to end abortion altogether."

The group has three locations: Altamonte Springs, Florida, Duluth Minnesota and St. Paul, Minnesota.

American Decency Association
AMERICANDECENCY.ORG

Founded in 1999, the American Decency Association (ADA) fights pornography and indecency in all its forms. Based in Fremont, Michigan, ADA was founded by former elementary school teacher Bill Johnson, who was the state director of the American Family Association from 1987 to 1999. ADA began as the Michigan chapter of the AFA, but Bill converted it to a stand alone ministry in 2000.

ADA's mission is "to educate its members and the general public on matters of decency; to initiate, promote, encourage and coordinate activity designed to safeguard and advance public morality consistent with biblical Christianity."

Over the years, ADA has teamed with other Christian groups in boycotts and campaigns to expose how corporate interests profit by peddling pornographic content. The ADA says its preferred tactic of choice for the ADA is letter-writing and threatening boycotts of advertisers and retailers who indirectly support indecent media.

Each week, Bill Johnson records several "A Decency Minute" radio spots discussing current issues which are aired on the American Family Network during various times around the country.

Salt & Light Council

SALTANDLIGHTCOUNCIL.ORG

Founded in 2008 by Dran Reese in Southern California, the Salt & Light Council (SLC) is a ministry tool for local churches and currently numbers about 80 congregations throughout the country.

SLC conducts workshops and provides training to establish Salt & Light Biblical Citizenship Ministries in churches offering education on worldview issues, along with ways people can advance constitutional and religious liberties, the sanctity of human life, marriage, family, and support for Israel.

Dran Reese, who continues to serve as President of SLC, is also a member of the Liberty Counsel Board of Directors. Several board members of Liberty Counsel have joined the SLC board, with Mat Staver serving as the Chairman of both boards. Together, Liberty Counsel and SLC have offices in Florida, California, Virginia, Washington, D.C., and Israel.

SLC helps people begin and sustain Salt & Light Biblical Citizenship Ministries at their churches, offering guidance, live and online training workshops and customizable, downloadable materials.

Florida Abolitionist

FLORIDAABOLITIONIST.ORG

Founded in Orlando by Tomas J. Laras, Florida Abolitionist is dedicated to stopping human trafficking, not the least of which is sex trafficking.

Human Trafficking is the fastest growing criminal activity in the world. It impacts people of all races, backgrounds, and nationalities, including in America. From kidnapping to parents willingly selling their children, from agricultural industries to local restaurants, human trafficking is aggressively taking hold. Amid this injustice and slavery, there is hope.

Florida Abolitionist believes it can and will end human trafficking in America, with a specific four-way plan:

Protection: As a First Responder in Central Florida, FA facilitates correct placement for each individual survivor.

Prosecution: As a victim-centered organization, FA's victim advocates provide support to clients who choose to testify against their trafficker.

Prevention: Educating, equipping, and empowering students, parents, and others to create healthy communities that are resistant to recruiting tactics of the traffickers.

Partnership: Florida Abolitionist is a catalyst for effective coalitions and task forces in collaboration with governmental and non-governmental organizations throughout Florida and the U.S.

Parents Television Council
W2.PARENTSTV.ORG

Founded in 1995 by conservative activist L. Brent Bozell III, who is founder and president of the Media Research Center, the Los Angeles-based Parents Television Council's mission is to "protect children and families from graphic sex, violence, and profanity in the media because of their proven long-term harmful effects." Tim Winters now serves as president of this invaluable ministry.

The group's vision is to "provide a safe and sound entertainment media environment for children and families across America."

Through publications on its website including staff reviews, research reports, and web-based newsletters, the Council judges whether television programs or other entertainment products benefit or harm children and works to encourage broadcasters and content producers to provide wholesome content.

Steve Allen, former host of "The Tonight Show," was PTC's Honorary Chairman and a member of its Advisory Board.

Special Olympics
SPECIALOLYMPICS.ORG

In 1962, Eunice Kennedy Shriver started an innovative summer camp for young people with intellectual disabilities at her home in suburban Washington, D.C. The goal was to see if these young people—most of whom lived in institutions—could participate in sports and physical activities. This was a revolutionary idea at the time.

In 1968, the first Special Olympics International Summer Games, modeled after the Olympics, was held in Chicago, with about 1,000 athletes with intellectual disabilities from the USA and Canada competing.

In the past decade, the Special Olympics' Unified Sports program has dramatically expanded, with the number of athletes with intellectual disabilities and Unified Sports teammates reaching 5.3 million. The 2011 Special Olympics World Summer Games were held in Athens, Greece, with more than 6,000 athletes from 170 countries taking part. In 2017, the Special Olympics World Winter Games were held in Graz and Schladming in Styria, Austria, the nation that was the site of the first Special Olympics World Games held outside the U.S.

Back2God

B2GOD.COM

A campaign of Orlando-based Dexter Sanders Ministries, the Back2God movement's goal is "to see Godly restoration of the United States of America and Abroad. To Cause an AWAKENING of God's elect, that they may be TRANSFORMED and EMPOWERED to IMPACT the social, political and spiritual climate of the United States America."

Dexter hosts a national radio show, Back 2 God Radio, which is part of the Urban Family Communications Network on American Family Radio every weekday at 5 p.m. to 6 p.m. Eastern.

The program "encourages everyday people to get back to God's morals, values, and principles in our spirituality, politics, economics, and social behavior."

Vision America

VISIONAMERICA.ORG

Founded in Texas by Pastor Rick Scarborough, Vision America (VA) engages, equips, and empowers pastors and people of faith to influence the culture through active civic involvement for spiritual awakening.

VA is now headed by John Graves, a pastor with a law degree from Texas Tech University School of Law.

VA offers free educational resources to pastors and people of faith to empower and mobilize them to action.

"We use the latest technology and detailed public data to analyze where to focus our resources to make the greatest impact at the most politically opportune times. We target our efforts to areas in which voter turnout or citizen engagement has been historically poor so that we can bring measurable change in outcomes and/or issues that concern our nation."

How are you currently giving back? In what ways can you help others through your success? God has given us the ability to create wealth so that His will may be established. As we Invest with Purpose, we need to make giving a crucial part of how we manage our God-given resources.

IMPORTANT INFORMATION

Purchase the e-book at
50% OFF

with the promo code: INVP5FF

" This book, *Invested with Purpose*, is way overdue and a must-read for every Christian who desires to honor God in every aspect of their lives... including their investments."

Mark A. Minnella, CFS, CFCA
President, Integrity Investors, LLC

A Ministry of Nehemiah Project International

ABOUT THE PUBLISHER

Nehemiah Publishing is an exclusive full-service publisher operated by Nehemiah Project International Ministries. Our mission is to produce and distribute kingdom-class content that enables us to build kingdom businesses globally.

Our services include:
- Writing and editing
- Cover design and illustrations
- ISBN and copyright registration
- Book layout and design
- Book marketing and distribution
- Printing
- Fulfillment
- Translation
- Author consultation and coaching

Book formats:
- Paperback
- Hardcover
- E-Book
- Audio Book
- Flash Drives

We are an exclusive publisher, hence, we only take on authors whose work is consistent with our mission and vision. To be considered for our services, please visit us at **NehemiahPublishing.com** and fill out a publishing services request form.

ABOUT NEHEMIAH PROJECT

Nehemiah Project International Ministries, Inc. is a business development and support organization that works in partnership with churches, marketplace ministries, educational institutions, associations, and individuals around the world. We provide comprehensive, transformational, Bible-based business education, training, and business coaching for Christian entrepreneurs and organizations.

MISSION

To build kingdom businesses globally.

VISION

To transform the marketplace with
the gospel of the Lord Jesus Christ one
entrepreneur at a time.

TRAINING   COACHING   ACCESS TO CAPITAL

For more information, visit us at **NehemiahProject.org**.

BIBLICAL
ENTREPRENEURSHIP
Principles | Practices | Planning

A proven system that thousands of entrepreneurs around the world have used to align their business with their values, increase their top and bottom line while making a kingdom impact.

We use our proprietary course materials along with some of the best business resources available.

PRINCIPLES
Ground your business in biblical truth

PRACTICES
Best business practices for efficiency and growth

PLANNING
Develop a growth plan that aligns your mission, values, and goals with your kingdom impact

- Identifying Opportunities
- Taking Calculated Risks
- Biblical Profit
- Biblical Economics
- Marketing and Sales from a Biblical Approach

- Innovation
- Biblical Management
- Business Financing
- Succession and Exit
- Developing a Kingdom Business Plan

For more information or to enroll, visit us at **BE-Executive.com**.

OTHER COURSES

For more information, visit us at **NehemiahProject.org**.

KINGDOM
BUSINESS COACHING

Kingdom Business Coaching™ (KBC) is the sister company of Nehemiah Project. KBC is an international business coaching and consulting practice that uses a proactive 360-degree coaching approach with various strategic tools and experienced coaches to help clients build healthy God-honoring relationships, build kingdom companies that align with their values, and grow their top and bottom line with kingdom impact.

OUR MISSION

Helping kingdom companies achieve transformational results.

OUR SERVICES

 Ask a Kingdom Business Coach

 Group Coaching

 Customized Coaching

 Elite Coaching

COACHING SYSTEM

Business Life Cycle	Scorecard	KBC Keys	Team Development
Strategy Development	Marketing & Sales	Systems & Innovation	Financial Development

For more information or to schedule a free initial consultation, visit us at **KingdomBizCoaching.com.**

The **Global Kingdom Investors Network**™ (GKIN) is an online investment matching service for qualified members of the Nehemiah E-Community™ who desire to raise debt or equity financing to grow their company. The goal of the network is to connect Biblical Entrepreneurs to kingdom impact investors and kingdom impact investors to quality, kingdom impact deals.

The GKIN hosts live and online Investors Forums with the purpose to introduce Biblical Entrepreneurs to investors and investors to kingdom impact opportunities.

For more information on how to raise money for your business or how to invest in kingdom companies visit our website: **GlobalKingdomInvesting.com**

NEHEMIAH E-COMMUNITY

Connecting
Biblical
Entrepreneurs
to resources,
and investors
to Kingdom
impact
opportunities

| LEARN | COACHING | CONNECT | COMMERCE | ACCESS FINANCIN |

The Nehemiah Entrepreneurship Community (E-Community™) is a comprehensive and robust online membership platform, providing entrepreneurs with quality biblically-integrated online business training, group coaching, and opportunities to connect and network with other Biblical Entrepreneurs from around the world who share their values. The E-Community™ allows access to investors through a Global Kingdom Investors Network™. The E-Community™ is a secure, shared-value, high-impact network of investors and entrepreneurs who provide innovative products and services, and are contributing to the transformation of communities and nations.

"Staying connected with my entrepreneur friends from around the world through the E-Community strengthened me." - René Villar

For more information, visit **www.n-ecommunity.com**.

OTHER RESOURCES

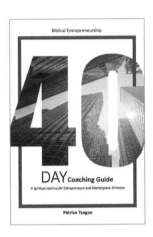